WORDS OF PRAISE FOR
SNAP OUT OF IT!

"**WE ALL NEED TO SNAP OUT OF IT** from time to time. This book shows you how to move from wherever you are-right there in your current experience-change gears and get into a groove with life."
>—**LORIN ROCHE, AUTHOR OF *MEDITATION MADE EASY,***
>***BREATH TAKING AND WHOLE BODY MEDITATIONS***

"**I HAVE TO ADMIT** this manuscript sat on the kitchen counter next to my smiley-face cookie jar for at least a week. 'Not again,' I was thinking, 'not another self-help brain jumble.' Was I ever relieved to discover this book is completely, totally, utterly different. Its genius is that it bypasses the mind, which acts like a strong-willed two-year-old most of the time, and cuts to the chase with the body and its senses where real change can occur.

"I love these unique exercises. The only drawback is my nine-year-old keeps rolling her eyes and wondering why mom is crawling on all fours, banging her chest like Tarzan and repeating 'Klaatu Barado Nikto' 25 times a day."
>—**PAM GROUT, AUTHOR OF *LIVING BIG, JUMPSTART YOUR***
>***METABOLISM, ART AND SOUL, AND GOD DOESN'T HAVE BAD HAIR DAYS***

"**THERE'S PLENTY OF INFORMATION AND INSPIRATION** in Ilene Segalove's book, *Snap Out of It,* if you're ready to change old habits and lifestyles that aren't working for you. Open her book to any chapter and you'll be both char~ ~ ~nd challenged to explore creative paths tow

>: **GOLDMAN, AUTHOR OF**
>:OMING A LATE BLOOMER

"**WITH WRY WISDOM AND INFECTIOUS MIRTH,** Ilene Segalove confirms the simple truth that life is too short to get stuck in a rut. Her 101 'snaps' are sure to rejuvenate your brain, restore your spirit, and reduce your stress. They will also make you laugh, think, and grow. Segalove's exercises are enlivened by fascinating facts and endearing anecdotes that may lead you to conclude that buzzing like a bumblebee and standing on your head are very smart—and healthy—things to do."

—**RICHARD MAHLER,** AUTHOR OF
STILLNESS: DAILY GIFTS OF SOLITUDE,
SECRETS OF BECOMING A LATE BLOOMER,
AND *TENDING THE EARTH, MENDING THE SPIRIT*

"**WHEN WE GET STUCK,** Ilene Segalove says we might 'try something different than what we are doing right now.' Simple advice, yet sound. Segalove provides an accessible alternative to the smiley-faced platitudes typically found in self-help books. *Snap Out of It* is a welcome relief from the tyranny of the positive attitude."

—**BARBARA HELD, PH.D.,** AUTHOR OF *STOP SMILING, START*
KVETCHING: A 5-STEP GUIDE TO CREATIVE COMPLAINING

SNAP
OUT OF IT!

101 ways to get out of your rut & into your groove

ILENE SEGALOVE

CONARI PRESS

First published in 2004 by
Red Wheel/Weiser, LLC
York Beach, ME
With offices at:
368 Congress Street
Boston, MA 02210
www.redwheelweiser.com

Library of Congress Cataloging-in-Publication Data

Segalove, Ilene.
Snap out of it : 101 ways to get out of your rut and into your groove
/ Ilene Segalove.
        p. cm.
Includes index.
  ISBN: 1-59003-061-3 (alk. paper)
  1. Self-actualization (Psychology) 2. Self-actualization
(Psychology)--Problems, exercises, etc. I. Title.
  BF637.S4S438 2004
  158.1--dc22

                                   2003015357

Typeset in Futura BT
Printed in the United States of America
RRD

11 10 09 08 07 06 05 04
 8 7   6   5   4   3   2   1

This snappy book is dedicated to
Snap Master and Cohort; man of many names
and faces—Pons Maar, Moustapha,
The Noid, Lead Wheeler, Roy Hess,
Hieronymous Ventriloquist, Thea's Dad,
Britta's Ex, Demetrios's and Lillian's Son,
and Thomas Michael Stamatelos.

Table of Contents

Acknowledgments

Snap wouldn't have been possible without the brilliance, heart, and expertise from the following eight humans: Gareth Esersky, Jan Johnson, Robyn Heisey Rowe, Julie Newendorp, Laurie Counihan-Childs, Camille Maurine, Lorin Roche, and Jude Bijou. Thank you.

Introduction

The Power of Snap

The movie *West Side Story* had just come out. I was a modern dancer and all the teenage girls in my after-school choreography class were crazy for the sound-track. Everyone wanted to play the lovely Maria in our upcoming amateur production—everyone except me. I wanted to be Riff, the head of the gang called the Jets, the oh-so-hip collection of boys that caused mayhem and danced sexy. I got the part! When it came time for the first rehearsal, I was scared. I had a great costume and knew all the words and most of the moves, but I couldn't figure out how to snap my fingers.

If you examine the fine art of snapping, you discover it isn't the finger placement that determines the quality of the "pop" so much as the pressure between the fingers. I was a good dancer but I must have had a major twist in the synapse that connects mind to matter. I just couldn't snap.

I practiced all the time. In the bathtub. Skipping to school. Dressing for bed. Watching TV. The house was haunted by my barely audible, poor excuse for finger snapping. The harder I tried, the worse it got. I simply could not get flesh and air to make the magic everyone else took for granted. Opening night came and I still hadn't mastered the snap. But, as someone once said, the show must go on.

I stood alone on a darkened stage in front of a few hundred people talking or snoring or rustling in their squeaky seats. The opening routine was meant to start in total silence. No lines. No music. Just eight crisp finger snaps. My teacher whispered, "Now!"

I snapped once. It was too soft. I snapped twice. My fingers sloppily slid off one another. I snapped again. This snap was loud! It was crisp! And that's when I learned the power of the snap. People seemed to snap out of their frenzy or stupor and actually woke up!

All eyes were now on me as I delivered my one line, "Let's get crackin', Daddy-O!" The curtain rose, the music swelled, and the spotlight lit up the slums of New York as a gaggle of girls, dressed up like Jets or Sharks, leapt and wiggled across the stage.

Forget Life and Get Back into Living

Humans are creatures of habit, and sometimes we get stuck in a rut. We can't step outside of our usual behavior, even when we know it's necessary for our mental health. Sometimes we're overwhelmed. We face a simple daily task and spin into panic or just plain freeze. We become spinners and wind ourselves into a tizzy or become zombies and space out in a stupor. Neither opens up our hearts or minds to the real challenges or pleasures at hand. We need to snap out of it and get back into living again. But how?

How many hours a day are you lost in a stupor or caught up in anxiety? Maybe it's time for you to break a habit, jump out of a pattern, and simply clean out your cobwebs instead of sweeping them under the rug. Maybe it's time for you to just snap out of it. Snap out of the "it" of being less than whole, fragmented, urgent, crazy, dull—zipping from one extreme to the other, not feeling right, not being your best self.

It's amazing how good it feels to drive out of the garage after an oil change and lube. The car runs a little more smoothly and feels a whole lot more responsive. We deserve the same kind of care. Just like cars, we humans need regular tune-ups.

Snap Out of It is an inquiry, a solution, and a total tune-up. It invites you to consciously stop, re-activate, regroup, and delight in being alive. It is a tonic of renewal and nourishment for your tired body, mind, and soul. Like patting your head and rubbing your belly at the same time, sensory combinations are life enhancing. (Didn't you know they had us do that in third grade to help us wake up and tune in?)

Our neurological systems thrive when we engage our five senses—sight, smell, touch/movement, sound, and taste. These 101 simple activities—based on childhood games, a little Chi Gung, some kinesiology, and a lot of innate know-how—challenge and delight our senses. Following these diverse, stimulating activities gives your zillions of brain neurons the green light to go ahead and build new networks of communication and expression. By unraveling our numerous knots of habit we can reawaken our spirit of play and bust out of our daily grind into a place of vitality, creativity, and ease.

Zombies and Spinners

Eastern thinking divides human behavior into two basic energetic profiles—yin and yang. Yin is a state of quiet receptiveness, filled with potential. Yang is the opposite style, filled with activity, busyness, and outward expression. Personal experience reflects a continual dance between the two ways of being. Most of us find ourselves inhabiting one state more than the other.

Zombies live in extreme yin. They handle life and its stresses by zoning out, getting dazed, spaced, or even paralyzed. Spinners live in extreme yang. They flip into manic obsession, are uptight, anxious, pent up, and overloaded. Zombies tend to run from life—that's called flight. Spinners tend to lash out at life—that's called fight. Our systems cannot tolerate either state for long before screaming, "Get yourself out of here!" Neither lethargy nor anxiety allows us to make good choices or enjoy ourselves. Both beg us, "Snap out of it!"

Who Are You?

Review the following keywords—anything sound familiar?

Zombie: Stupor. Lethargy. Spaced. Frozen. Fear. Paralyzed. Depressed. Down. Unable to feel or care. Quiet. Internal. Flight. Loose and shapeless. Wants to disappear. Needs to activate.

Spinner: Manic. Anxious. Nervous. Overwhelmed. Obsessive. Predatory. Spun out. Up. Loud. External. Fight. Panic. Tightly wound. Unable to focus or manifest. Wants to explode. Needs to relax.

Roadmaps of Living

Humans are billions of individual cells arranged in an infinite array of different patterns that organize themselves into our very unique being. Your hand is a set of patterns. So are your liver and your uvula. Your brain also expresses itself as different patterns. It creates its own set of networks in response to stimuli and repeated actions. Networks are neural off-ramps onto ways of doing and being. When we use these off-ramps over and over again, we fall into habit. Our most habitual roadmaps become etched in our brain circuitry and become guidelines for our behavior.

Yet the brain is considered a plastic medium. It can change shape, and does. Adult brains refashion themselves according to the demands of the owner. It's like we're all the heads of our own department of roadwork—if we want to stop traveling the same old Main Street over and over again, we need to build new freeways and bridges and tunnels.

Creatures of Habit

Of course, many of our habits are so ingrained we fail to recognize how robotic we have become. It's all autopilot. On one hand, it's great—how wonderful that we don't have to concentrate on walking as our legs habitually carry us across the room. But on the other hand, if we succumb to this robotic behavior, our ingenuity becomes sluggish, almost knee-jerk, and we deny ourselves so many options.

There's an old Spanish proverb: "Habits at first are like silken threads. Then they become cables." It's important to develop rituals and routines to make life flow. But when routines turn into ruts, or tie us down, we need help getting out.

Fight or Flight

Getting stuck is a form of stress and stress is a reaction to a perceived threatening situation. When anything tips the scale toward threat, we humans automatically flip into fight or flight. Our body is hardwired to either fight (Spinners) or flee (Zombies). We don't even need to experience big or real danger. If we just think about an emotional or physical threat, all kinds of powerful bodily reactions kick in. Our heart beats faster. Our breathing rate and blood pressure increases. Our hands and feet become cooler to shunt blood from the extremities to the big muscles so that we can fight or run with some success. Even the pupils in our eyes dilate so we can see better.

The reptilian brain, the oldest part of our brain, spends most of its time asking, "Am I safe?" Our lives are no longer in constant peril, but most of us are consistently on the lookout while casually reading a book, sipping tea, or balancing our checkbook. We may perceive a serious threat while simply sitting silently at our desks. Maybe we get a nasty e-mail from someone we don't like. Those forty little electronic words can blast our systems into active red alert. Our ancient soul screams "Danger!" We become a house divided. Running on automatic, we flip into manic and start pacing and sweating (Spinners). Or maybe we space out, freeze and go numb (Zombies). There's no visible monster in sight, but, again, that doesn't seem to matter. This isn't about what makes sense. This is core. This is survival!

Fight or flight puts us through some serious paces. Since our bodies house vital electrical and chemical systems that percolate day and night, there's bound to be a lot of action. Our brains are filled with busy circuits housing thousands upon thousands of signals. But just like cell phone switching stations, our internal switchers can become jammed or confused, especially when we're on red alert. This is a key moment. We all know when we're starting to spin or space. A red alert means, "Snap out of it."

What Do I Do Now?

If you've ever had a dog you know the feeling you get when you see him spinning in circles as he chases his tail. At first it is amusing. But as he spins and spins and seems to be digging a hole deep into the carpet you start to worry. He may not stop. You recognize he's in some kind of ancient genetic loop. You feel the need to intervene. You offer him a ball or a cookie. You try to distract him. Or you yell loudly, "Stop it!" hoping you can scare him out of his stupor. Once he stops, he may look at you like, "What the heck was I doing? Phew. Thanks." When habit has gotten you by the tail, stop spinning, pick up *Snap Out Of It*, and find your way back into life again.

I come from years of feeling the pressure of time. My parents were both avid clock-watchers. They spent most of the day getting direction from their matching Timex wrist watches. We lived in a combustible, if imaginary, 911 world. As I got older, I embodied emergency room behavior. I was my own sergeant, shouting directions, ordering myself around. Whether I was cooking or gardening or even taking a bath, I got these weird urges to rush. Quick, sauté those onions! Quick, pull those weeds! Quick, wash your face! Anxious and pooped out, I found myself often disconnected from enjoying or even engaging in the task at hand.

When I get stuck, I need a break. I need to remember I'm safe. And I need to admit I'm falling into habit again. I may pace, drink coffee, make some phone calls, even vacuum. But if nothing snaps me out of it, what do I do? I check right into a favorite activity, Sacred Password (#60, page 122). I extend my arms and gaze upward. I like to repeat out loud, "It's all okay. I'm doing the best I can," instead of a conventional prayer. Immediately I sense a real change. You see, conscious movement is groundbreaking. First, I'm taking a moment to snap out of it. I'm not pushing the red alert sign away, but I'm handling it in my own way. I know there is nothing to run away from or to fight. The alarm system is teaching me something more. It's reminding me I have a choice!

One day I found myself skimming the newspaper and starting to feel deeply uneasy. Instead of surrendering to depression and taking a nap I snapped out of it by trying out Wild Hoots (#22, page 52). I started to growl like a tiger. Then, since I felt like a caged animal, I acted like one and paced in my make-believe cage. After a few minutes I tried Kick It (#4, page 24), moved some static energy, felt much better, wiggled and growled, and then nestled back into my chair. I found myself paying attention, at last. Refocused and refreshed, I realized I had probably just looked and sounded pretty crazy. But had I lost my mind? Not really. I actually found it. I snapped out of my basic ancient brain and got current and conscious at last.

Let's say you're writing on the computer (or reading, or working out a math problem) and you get stuck. You're instantly spaced (Zombie) or anxious (Spinner). Quick! Flip through *Snap Out of It!* and circle a few activities that jump off the page. The good news is that all 101 activities will pick you up or settle you down, depending on what your system needs at the moment.

For example, if you're spaced and need to revitalize, the Belly Breather Stress Buster (#54, page 109) will shift you into alertness. But if you're pent up and needing relaxation, the same activity will calm you down. Your system knows what it needs.

Maybe you'll Yawn Big & Loud (#17, page 44), bend Upside Down (#50, page 99), and discover what's been sitting behind you all these years. Perhaps you'll settle down by putting Head to Earth (#56, page 112). In no time, and with very little effort, you'll rewire your neurological circuits, take a breather, and grow a new point of view. Relaxed and centered, you'll be ready to move past the specter of fatigue or urgency to reengage with life.

Break out of your stupor. Get out of your trance. Bust the spell of tired old patterns. Interrupt the humdrum. Turn off the automatic pilot and shape-shift into a new point of view. Shine brighter. Feel lighter. Expand your vistas. Sigh. Laugh. Relax. Rejoice. Know you have a choice. Reconnect to life again simply by taking a break. Look out the window. Listen to the wind. Sing a song. Make your mark. Twist and shout. And put your genie in a bigger bottle!

Put Your Genie in a Bigger Bottle

I overheard a conversation on a flight from Atlanta to Los Angeles. It was between a magician and a chemist. The chemist said he had concocted a formula that successfully cleaned all surfaces, real or synthetic. The magician said, "So you're an alchemist."

The chemist said, "No."

The magician pulled a coin from behind the chemist's ear. "Now you say you clean all surfaces, both real and unreal. And you say you brew potions in a laboratory. Sounds like magic to me."

The chemist got nervous. "That's not magic. I'm essentially a businessman. Just like you. We're all trying to make a living. Nothing more." The chemist frantically dug into his briefcase and pulled out a Walkman, headphones, and a Palm Pilot. He plugged in as a glazed look filled his eyes and instantly zoned out.

"You are not listening to me," the magician insisted. He leaned into the chemist's left ear and whispered, "Put your genie in a bigger bottle."

The chemist pulled off his headphones. "What?"

"Unplug yourself. Crack yourself open. And snap out of it. You'll be amazed to discover who you really are."

"Hocus pocus," the chemist sneered.

"Abracadabra," the magician announced.

"Open sesame," I chimed in.

And then there was a crackling sound and the pilot announced, "Just a simple electrical failure, folks. Nothing to worry about. We'll get things shipshape in no time." The headsets went dead, the movie had frozen, and the reading lamps fizzled out. Everyone squirmed in their seats as the scent of fear and disconnect floated down the aisles.

I gazed over at the chemist. Somehow, in the darkness, his face transformed from anxiety to delight. It was as if the power failure snapped him out of the prison of habit into a place of choice. It was remarkable how totally different he seemed, like Pinocchio when he transformed from wooden puppet to real boy. He came alive, leaped up, and patted the magician on the back. The magician laughed loudly and then the two of them, as though led by a shared but silent call, walked over to a window and eagerly gazed out at the vast and perfectly blue sky.

How to Use This Book

Snap Out of It is a collection of 101 mini-adventures, playful explorations, and simple acts of discovery that will help you snap out of habit to get back into living life more fully. Dip into the following eight chapters filled with stories, activities, and more whenever you are stuck on a particular problem, lost in a mood, or just want to get a fresh perspective. If you are pressed for time, try Quick Snaps. These snappy activities are printed in bold headlines that jump right off the page! If you want to explore your creativity a little, take a peek at the Snap To Your Imagination exercises that thread throughout each chapter.

Just remember that there is no right or wrong way to snap out of it. The whole idea is to simply try something different than what you are doing right now.

Guaranteed, you will dive back into the game more alert, more at ease, and with more choices up your sleeve.

Three Easy Ways to Get Started

1. Flip through the book. Close your eyes if you wish and randomly open to a page, any page. Read the activity chance has chosen for you and spend at least one full minute trying it out.

2. Read through the entire book from start to finish and circle all of the activities that speak to you. Then try them out in any order you wish.

3. If you need something special to help you snap out of a particular state of mind, go directly to chapter 8: The Last Eleven—Mix and Match 'Em. Ask yourself out loud, "What do I need to do right now?" If you don't know, take a big breath and ask again. "What do I need?" Trust your intuition and choose the combo that tickles your fancy. If, for example, you need to get going, check out the Energizing Combo (#92, page 177). If you need to take a break try the Relaxing Combo (#91, page 177).

Or Get Started by Checking Out Your Sensory Preference

The five key senses—sight, movement or touch, sound, smell, and taste—are doorways into discovering and enjoying our world. One great way to snap out of it is to determine your habitual sensory orientation, the one dominant sense that seems to rule the roost. As babies, we tended to use all five of our senses equally. When we entered preschool, our brains began to identify more strongly with one sense than with the others. Over time we began to feel most comfortable performing activities and inhabiting environments that provided for this sensory preference. It's natural to want to express who we are in our perceived sensory preference. When we create an activity that matches our sensory preference, we feel "together," validated, confident, and successful. But we can also get dulled out in this comfort zone. Exploring an activity that challenges you in a new sensory orientation is guaranteed to help you snap out of it quickly and easily.

What is your personal sense orientation? Consider how you take in information from the outside world. What type of sensory stimuli gets your attention most quickly? Although there are five key senses, sensory preferences are broken down into three main categories. Are you kinesthetic (movement and touch)? Or are you auditory, or visual? Some studies suggest approximately 60 percent of the population has a visual sensory preference, 20 percent is auditory, and 20 percent is kinesthetic. You'll know which you are by reviewing the following brief profiles:

With a **kinesthetic** preference your brain relates to touch, taste, temperature, and odors most quickly. You are sensitive to your environment, finding comfort in the textures of furniture, nature, and physical touch.

If you have an **auditory** preference, your brain relates to sound stimuli most quickly. You tend to learn a lot about a situation by the tone of someone's voice or other sounds that catch your attention. You also resonate with the joy of written communication and are often an active listener. Music and speech are a big part of your natural self-expression. By the same token, you are often very sensitive to noise.

If you have a **visual** preference, your brain relates to visual stimuli most quickly. You probably crave attractive surroundings, often like stylish and colorful clothing, and probably enjoy watching movies, TV, animals, and anything that moves. You absorb information about the environment through the way things look and usually prefer face-to-face conversations rather than phone calls or e-mail.

It makes "sense" to determine your sensory preference. Once you do, you can easily choose one of the 101 activities that either supports or challenges your comfort zone. Check out the chapter titles. You'll notice chapter 1 speaks to the kinesthetic. Chapter 2 is auditory and chapter 3 is visual. The rest are combinations, of course. If you are a visual person try an activity that stimulates a totally different way of being—explore movement and dive into chapter 1. Or experiment with sound and check out chapter 2. You'll be amazed how quickly you snap out of it when you crack open the possibilities of being your best and biggest self.

Twist

and

Shout

1—MAKE A FACE

Wrinkle up your face. You know, nose crunched up, eyes squished, mouth puckered. Make all those hideous and fantastic expressions you haven't indulged in for years.

Open your jaws real wide, stick out your tongue, and bug out your eyes. Be grotesque, funny, and extreme. Engage your face in a raging romp and try on expressions of disgust, surprise, laughter, horror, and total delight.

Beauty Regime

My grandmother was really fastidious. She always folded her clothes with newspapers in between the arms and torso to keep them in perfect alignment. She removed all lint with a Magic Wand roller and hand ironed all of her collars and cuffs. One of my favorite memories is of watching her put on makeup.

I would sit on the cushy black rug on the bathroom floor and gaze up as she "put on her face." First she'd pucker up her lips and pull back her mouth ten times like some exotic fish. With some natural glow pulsing through her porcelain skin, she'd know exactly where to pat the loose powder which waited for her in a lovely golden box. Next she'd frown and smile really fast, and then it was time to pencil in her eyebrows. That's when I'd get up and choose the color of her rouge and lipstick. She'd congratulate me on my choices and then grab my hands. We'd spin our eyes in circles, wrinkle up our noses, and hold our breath together.

After that we'd let out one long sigh, in unison. She'd curl her eyelashes, whisk on mascara, and outline and paint in her lips. Rouge was last and best. It highlighted her high cheekbones and made her look like a just-picked perfect apple. One final glance in the mirror and she'd say, "How do I look?" I'd say, "Beautiful," and then we'd kick up the rug and waltz across the pink tile floor.

At night my grandmother would rub Vaseline all over her face. She'd cover her eyes with a black silk mask and set the alarm for four in the morning. Every dawn she'd get up in the dark and sip lemon juice with hot water. I guess she knew what she was doing, because when my grandmother died, she didn't have a single wrinkle, and she looked really happy.

 **MORE...**

The human face has the most complex and highly-developed set of facial muscles in the entire animal world. Most of us use only a tiny fraction of our potential expressiveness, dipping into a few habitual "faces" to fit all of life's dramas. The simple, safe smile. The critical scowl. The raised eyebrow smirk. Our faces tend to lock into habitual expressions as if we're afraid to try something new—like the way we have five hundred CDs but play the same four crowd pleasers over and over, for every occasion.

Many human expressions are barely perceptible, because they come and go in less than a second, but you can train yourself to sense them and tune into what they tell you. As you do so, you will find a rich world of meaning you never knew existed.

Sometimes faces become masks, handy cover-ups that hide instead of reveal true feelings. Our faces suffer as they are locked into habit. The many muscles that are never worked lose their tone, and the ones that are overused freeze or wrinkle up.

Each day, extend the range of your facial expressions. Work your facial muscles. Working muscles creates good blood flow and tones the skin. It massages your senses organs: nose, eyes, tongue, mouth, ears. And it feels good too.

2—SHAKE IT OUT

Stand with your feet shoulder width apart, arms hanging loosely at your sides. Now gently bounce. Don't pick up your feet—wiggle or roll around on your heels and toes. You are a rag doll. Get loose. Let your arms dangle, your neck bop, your shoulders float up and down. You are a marionette. Increase the speed and intensity. After a few minutes, slow down and find your balance again.

 MORE...

When we focus on a task for more than a few minutes, we often forget to move our bodies. They cramp up, numb out, or even seem to disappear. We end up feeling like some giant head floating in space with no body at all, like some skin-encapsulated ego with lots of ideas but no arms or legs. This reaction mirrors the way fear grips our bodies. When we are afraid or overwhelmed, we freeze.

When we aren't moving, our muscles and emotions become rigid. Like petrified wood, where the malleable softwood actually turns to stone, we stiffen and feel a little dead, disembodied, and disconnected from ourselves and the world around us.

Whether you are scared or just stuck in a pattern, shaking it out helps you reconnect and get grounded.

A few minutes of dedicated shaking invigorates your heart, breath, and emotions—it gets your juices flowing. At the same time, you'll shake out that rigidity before it sinks into your bones. You will end up feeling both calm and rejuvenated at the same time.

If you want to learn how to shake really well, watch ducks. They are master shakers. After a fight or some momentary conflict, they shake their feathers from head to toe, get the stiffness quickly out of their systems, and quack on.

QUICK SNAP

3—JUMP UP AND DO THE HULA!

4—KICK IT

Stand up and just start kicking. Put some gusto into it! Kick the air, pretend to kick someone you are angry at, kick an invisible sand bag. Let one leg snap out and back over and over again, then switch to your other leg. Kicking loosens up your knees and releases pent-up energy. Stomp your feet when you are done.

Float Tank

Float tanks are strange but wonderful stress-relief devices and were all the rage in the late seventies. They are lightproof, soundproof, fiberglass tubs, half filled with a saline solution. You climb in, lower the lid, and float with no distractions.

I decided to try one out. I put on a headset, slid into the tank, closed my eyes, and tried to get comfortable. It was a little scary and claustrophobic at first, but someone pumped music through my headset and after about ten minutes, I began to relax. As I hovered in a slightly altered state for at least an hour, my body slowly unwound. All of the tension of standing and sitting and walking and grappling with gravity seemed to unpeel itself. As I tripped in and out of daydreams, I could feel the muscles in my neck unravel and my hands loosen their grip.

Most of the time I felt as though I was buoyantly hovering in an empty black night sky. Every now and then I'd see what looked like a shooting star flicker across my vision. I realized it was the image my optic nerve concocted every time some part of me gave in. Shoulders dropped. Shooting star. Jaw unclenched. Shooting star. It was so beautiful to give in to the warmth and security of this pseudo-sea and literally watch myself melt.

I scanned my body and realized every inch of my being had happily dissolved into the water except for my quadriceps. My thighs, the muscles that always work, and never hurt, just couldn't, just wouldn't give in. But why? My noodle brain wrapped around this riddle for a moment and then the night sky revealed a big brown ball rolling toward me. I was on my grammar school playground standing in the center of the kickball ring. I got the sense that something was missing. And then I realized that somewhere along the way I forgot how to kick. I squirmed inside the tank. How long had it really been? How long had I been holding all that energy back? Without thinking further, I began kicking in the water. Kicking hard. So hard the lid popped open and crashed onto the floor. So hard that water splashed all over the room and the manager of the facility rushed in to see what all the racket was.

I climbed out and stood there grinning. Saline was dripping off my body. "I got such a kick out of the tank. Sorry," I apologized. The manager looked annoyed. "It happens a lot," he told me. "Go home and find yourself a ball."

 MORE...

Sometimes an unsettling phone call or long line at the bank gets us unnerved and angry, but instead of moving to unwind we freeze and fume. Our necks get tight and our lower backs lock. We hold all this pumped-up energy in our bodies.

Our minds are wired to fight or flight. Our bodies are still built to respond to saber-tooth tigers. We get a nasty e-mail and respond like the tiger is coming after us...but...there is no tiger. Still we are ready to go. It's time to kick and stomp.

Kicking is a form of running without having to run. No need to put on your shoes and headband—just get up and fire away. You'll move. You'll breathe. You'll recover. By loosening your knees and letting your body know it's in action, you'll find the instinct to run diminishes and within a few minutes you'll feel a sense of relief and calm wash over you.

 SNAP TO YOUR IMAGINATION

5—TREE TIME

Pretend you are a tree. Your feet are rooted into the ground, being fed by the nutrients deep within the earth. Imagine your arms are branches growing out of your body, pulling you into the sky. You are sturdy. You connect earth and heaven and stand proud, a vertical pose of beauty and fearlessness. Stand and sway like a favorite tree. You are balance.

Life is movement. Movement is life. It is expression in form. As we move, we are constantly reshaping our vision, picking up sounds and scents, and interacting with our rich sensory environments.

Movements are very personal expressions of who we are. They are a natural way to keep in touch with other people and the world. Our sedentary lives contribute to our bodies becoming storehouses of tension instead of expressions of vitality.

We are meant to process life, not keep it frozen. Twist and shout and revitalize and restore.

6—CROSSWALK

Stand up and march in place. Now alternately touch your right hand to your left knee and your left hand to your right knee, crossing over the midline of your body. Get a nice momentum going. If you want, walk around the room like this. Or sit down and continue the crosswalk.

 MORE...

When you do any movement that crosses the midline of the body you are activating both of your brain hemispheres simultaneously. Movements of coordination stimulate our auditory, visual, and kinesthetic aptitudes and improve our ability to listen, read, and retain information.

7—Spinning Windmill

Stand up, bend your knees, and lean forward. Look at a place about one yard in front of your feet. Dangle your arms and swing them loosely. Let them be heavy. Now rotate your knees and hips, allowing your arms to follow on either side of your body.

Imagine a windmill. Inhale and circle your arms backwards for seven counts. Then exhale and circle your arms forward for three counts. The balance of the breath and the direction of the arms are important. It might take a little while to coordinate. Try a few sets. You'll discover the momentum will carry you into the movement. It's fun. As you slow down, end on the exhale, circling forward.

 MORE...

The energizing windmill loosens your muscles and ligaments and opens up your joints, moving your energy up and around. Don't worry if your fingers tingle a bit—you're just a little more alive than a few minutes ago. The body is a spiral shape, not a stick figure.

This move recreates the spiral of your structure and allows you to feel a connection with the ground and your center. It also affects the pH balance in your bloodstream (pH is the ratio between the acid and alkaline content of our bodies). When we are too acidic we feel sad or depressed. Too much alkaline makes us feel exhilarated but a tad manic. Doing the Spinning Windmill will rebalance your acid/alkaline ratio, leading you to a feeling of clarity and wellbeing.

8—ROCKABY BABY

Sit down and cradle yourself in your own arms. Wrap your arms around your shoulders or hug your waist— whatever feels right. Begin rocking forward and backward, moving from the middle of your body up. Be soft and gentle. Find yourself moving in small circles, clockwise and then counterclockwise.

 MORE...

This movement is so natural. You'll recognize it as something you've done before, maybe when you were a child. If it helps soothe a screaming baby, it should quiet your adult body too. It's an almost automatic way we respond to grieving or suffering. It helps us to rediscover our center. You may discover rocking actually encourages tears, or a big sigh of relief. Even if you aren't upset, doing Rockaby Baby gives you a sense of comfort and release.

9—ON ALL FOURS

Crawl on the floor on all fours. You did it years ago—and probably rather well. Crawling will come back to you pretty quickly and feels good. Give it a shot.

Sweet Potato Whip

It was Thanksgiving. I had promised my famous sweet potato whip, a yummy blend of orange potatoes, apple juice, and cinnamon. I poured the concoction into a large glass bowl, dabbed a few slices of butter on top, and popped it into the oven to turn a delicious golden brown. This holiday dinner party was tiny—just me, my best friend, her brother, and his best friend, who was a rescue parachute jumper from the Air Force. All I knew about him was that he had black hair and pointy ears, and resembled Spock from Star Trek. I was instantly attracted to him.

The duck was roasting and smelled really good. I had my head in the oven when this terribly handsome man walked into the kitchen and said, "Hello, Isadora." My name is Ilene, but I loved how his voice sounded as he called me something so exotic. I spun around, we locked eyes, and I pulled the bubbling sweet potato whip out of the oven. I set it on top of the oven as he inhaled deeply and smiled. "Yum."

We all took our places and clicked our goblets in a toast. I lifted the bubbly, eager to take a sip, but the moment it wet my lips, there was this horrible, loud sound from the kitchen. The sweet potato whip had literally exploded. There was golden yellow mush everywhere, sprinkled with tiny pieces of shredded glass. (Apparently, the dish I used only looked like oven-friendly Pyrex—as the sweet potato whip cooled off, the glass cracked.)

Instead of impressing Spock with my domestic talents, I found myself crawling on all fours, cleaning potato and glass from the walls and floor. He crawled on hands and knees, too, not minding creasing his corduroys as he followed close by, laughing softly—and sweetly—at my mistake.

MORE...

When we crawl, the spine is suspended like a hammock, supported by four springy "legs." Crawling does more than trigger both sides of the physical body so that they can work harmoniously. It also activates speech and language centers of the brain and stimulates integrative learning.

An interesting fact supports the value of crawling on all fours: When 100 centenarians were interviewed to determine what kept them alive and well, crawling once a day was at the top of the list, right underneath a daily shot of scotch and doing crossword puzzles.

 SNAP TO YOUR IMAGINATION

10—POWER ANIMAL

Pretend you are one of your favorite animals or insects. Shape-shift from one creature to the next as you stretch, shudder, wiggle, stalk. Mimic animals that crawl, swim, hunt, fly, and burrow. Discover comfort in your own skin.

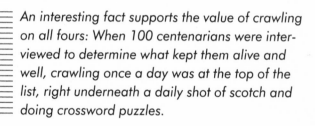

11—FIGHT CLUB

Raise your left arm straight up into the air. Allow it to hover a moment, lined up alongside your head. Now take your left hand and place it on your right upper arm muscle (biceps). Resist with your left hand as you push forward isometrically with your right arm. Count to eight. Now move your right arm against resistance in three other directions: toward the back wall, toward your ear, and away from your ear. Count to eight for all moves and then repeat the sequence on the other side.

 MORE...

This is a powerful form of muscle activation. It involves lengthening the sides of your body and gives your arms room to fire without hurting anybody. And it relaxes and coordinates the shoulder and arm muscles. If you are pent up, confined, or even angry, and you don't express it with a strong right hook, it can lock up the muscles in the shoulder socket. This tension builds and then you feel stuck and frustrated. So activate your fighting arms and release whatever is lurking.

12—Yes Master, No Master

Sit down for this one so you can focus on the sensations without getting dizzy. Cross your arms in front of your chest, elbows bent at ninety-degree angles, arms parallel to the ground. Place the right palm on top of the left bent elbow and the top of the left hand under the right elbow. They are stacked and resemble the Hollywood image of the genie, always ready to serve.

Now nod "Yes" very slowly. Let your head drop down and then glide back up. Continue the movement of the head backwards until it is tilted upwards, and then repeat. Say the word "Yes" to yourself. Do this as slowly as you can, paying attention to the sense of motion. Then speed up the movement to your ordinary "nodding yes" speed.

Nod "No" and think no, as you vigorously shake your head back and forth. Then slow the movement down and feel it through and through.

 MORE...

Nodding up and down for "yes" and sideways for "no" is not universal. In India, for example, vertical head-nodding can mean yes or no, depending on where you come from on the continent. Head rocking, turning, and drawing a figure eight in the air with your chin can mean yes, maybe, or no, or any shade of meaning in-between. In Bulgaria, Greece, and Turkey, nodding the head up and down means no, not yes.

No and yes are the basic - and +, the yin and yang of communication. They are powerful statements of acceptance or rejection. If you are unable to fully express either or both, then your life will be limited. Your relationships and your ability to care for yourself will be impaired. Every person needs to have at least ten ways of saying yes, from a quiet acknowledgment to a completely enthusiastic embrace and confirmation. Have you ever noticed how good it feels to say no to something you really do not want? Every person needs ten levels of no, from a quiet, reflective, "No, I don't think I will," to a completely emphatic, absolute, "No!"

And remember that when you say no and mean it, you are actually saying yes to your truth.

13—You Are a Statue

Stand up and slowly turn in a circle. Vary your tempo. To keep from getting dizzy, spot an object in the room and keep your eyes focused on it as you spin around. If you wish, begin to circle the other way. Now stop and freeze in one position. Recreate a famous pose, like Rodin's

The Thinker, the Statue of Liberty, or the seated smiling Buddha. Whatever you do, don't move. Turn to marble for a moment.

 MORE...

Spinning is a paradoxical way of finding apparent stillness inside of movement. Think about the quiet eye of a hurricane. Whirling dervishes spin to find the quiet center within chaos. Sometimes they close their eyes. Sometimes they focus on their thumb as they spin with arms outstretched.

Moving opens up your energy. As you explore spinning, stop thinking, lose your head, and let go of everything outside of you. Spinning invites you to rely on your inner senses instead of depending on your overly dominant eyes. Imagine the rotation of the galaxies, planets, and atoms. Swirl yourself free from everything that tries to grab you. Move into a place where conflicts are held in meaningful wholeness.

And then stop. Freeze. Feel your body-shape, the relative position of limbs, torso, and head. If you saw yourself from the outside, what would you see? Is there poetry in your pose? What tone is in your gesture? Emotionally sensing what the statue shape evokes gives you a clue to your inner feelings. Now focus on the heightened inner sensations of all that energy.

Scars

I spun across the backyard like a fairy. Then I dove onto the glider on the old metal swing set, swung back and forth, and jumped off like a fantastic action figure. I was Peter Pan. One day I leaped off and posed like a winner after beating Captain Hook in a nasty sword fight. But I missed my footing. My statuesque moment was shattered as the glider rammed into my collarbone. I got this big, ugly bruise. When I dashed into the house, my mother spotted it and shrieked, "Oh my God. You're scarred for life. Now you'll never be able to wear low-cut evening gowns."

In a few days the swelling and redness disappeared, and in a couple of weeks it turned into a small pink and white scar, about the size of a quarter. It liked it. I thought it added character to my bland, eight-year-old body. My mother was still upset. "It's such a shame," she lamented, "You were perfect up till now."

14—Facedown Touchdown

Get down on the floor
and lie face down.
Make a pillow with your
hands and nestle your

head. Spread your legs out as wide as you like and
press your belly, breasts, thighs, and pubic bone into
the rug. Make contact with the earth. Drop your
weight and relax. Wiggle from side to side, and feel
how your hips move with a rhythmic momentum.
After a few minutes you may notice you seem to fit
into the floor, as if the curve of the earth is molding
and reaching up to hold you. Take a nice rest.

 MORE...

Our underbelly is usually hidden or protected. As you
sink into the floor and release, your viscera silently
sigh and gladly give in. Gravity shifts the way your
insides hang together, and liver, spleen, stomach, and
intestines rejoice a little as they get to drop forward.

The belly is considered the center of the body in many
cultures. It is also designated as a major energy
center that governs the mental and emotional issues
of self-esteem, trust, personal honor, accomplish-
ment, and how we present ourselves to the world.
Lying on your belly is a way of supporting and recon-
necting with this powerful place. There is often a kind
of emotional release that comes when you face belly

to the ground. And even though the planet is traveling one thousand and thirty eight miles an hour at the equator while orbiting around the sun, our Mother Earth still provides a solid place to land and seek comfort. She may pull out some tears along the way, but your heaviness and anxiety will soon lighten.

15—ON THE RIGHT FOOT

Find a corner of the room where you have something to hold onto. With bare feet, stand on both legs and imagine you are standing on sand. Let one foot float

off the ground. Be careful, not too high. Wait awhile, then change legs. Now do the same thing with your eyes closed. You may need to hold onto the wall or a chair for support.

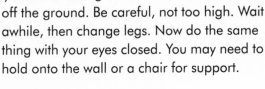 **MORE...**

In every movement, with every function, there is a fluid balance which wanders between the weight sinking through your feet and the head pressing up into the air. Bearing down into the ground is really a way of standing up. Be mindful of the flow of energy toward the heavens while remembering the simultaneous flow toward the earth.

As you balance, notice how your entire foot, all twenty-six bones and thirty-three articulations, makes contact with the floor. Pay attention to how your weight bears down, toes spread, and leg stiffens. Standing is not stillness. It is perpetual movement. Balancing on one foot illuminates how nothing is static. Tall trees are always swaying in some fashion.

Keeping your balance isn't only about your feet. It is also a function of your inner ear. Tiny bones and sacs of fluid and receptor hair cells do an intricate dance to keep you upright. The simple act of balancing not only activates your muscles, skeleton, brain, ears, and eyes, but stimulates your emotions as well. It is embarrassing to stumble while trying to balance on one foot—but once you reclaim your feet and remind them to wake up, they will be more like reliable roots, growing into the ground below, giving you a sense of solidity and stability.

QUICK SNAP

16—MARCH IN PLACE

Now March Outside and Slam the Door!

CHAPTER 2

All

Ears

17—YAWN BIG AND LOUD

Open up your mouth and yawn. Make
sounds with your breath and your
voice. Let your mouth wiggle around
until you find yourself yawning naturally. As you yawn lightly press your
fingertips against any tight spots
where your cheeks cover your upper and lower back
teeth. With tiny circular motions, stroke away any tension you uncover as you make a deep relaxed yawning sound. You may be momentarily sleepy. Ahhhh....

 MORE...

People aren't the only ones who yawn. Watch a cat or
dog get ready for a nap, and you'll probably see it
take a gigantic yawn as its mouth opens wide and its
tongue pops out. Even unborn babies are known to
yawn. No one knows the real scoop behind why we
yawn, but science calls it a low-intensity form of dis-
placement sleeping. It's a way to rest without going to
bed. When you are bored or tired you may not
breathe as deeply as you usually do. Your body takes
in less oxygen because your breathing has slowed. So
when you yawn, you bring more oxygen into the blood
and pull more carbon dioxide out. And yawning helps
relax the strong joint of the jaw—more than 50 percent of the neurological connections from the brain
must pass through here to get to the rest of the body.

Yawning never looks as good as it feels. But it is a great way of stretching from the inside out. Your eyes, your whole face, throat, chest, arms, and heart seem to relish the big natural swoop of increased circulation and stimulation. And yawning seems to be contagious. If you yawn in class or on the bus, you'll probably notice a few other people yawning, too. Even thinking about yawning can get you yawning. How many times have you yawned while reading this?

SNAP TO YOUR IMAGINATION

18—TIME TRAVELER

Pretend you are in the future. Now think back on the present moment. What would you have done differently? Answer out loud. So, what are you waiting for? Do it. You are on top of it. You are true.

19—EAVESDROP

Listen to the sounds of your house. Wander through your home and slow down your pace. Move in circles rather than straight lines. This will enhance your ability to gather sound and will sharpen your listening. Any clocks ticking? Is someone cooking or brushing their teeth? Go down to the basement or near the garage and listen to the sizzling of your electric circuit breakers. Notice the subtle beating rhythm of your water heater. Pretend your ear is a giant receiver and be attentive.

Elvis in Paint

I dreamt I was swimming in my childhood bedroom. There was no water, but that didn't matter. I swam so fast I hit my head on the ceiling. Some of the colored plaster crackled down onto the carpet and set off a shock wave that grew outward, spreading wildly until it hit the nearby walls. As the ceiling crumbled, it seemed to transform from solid to liquid and melted in mid-air, turning into a thick, yellow paint. Then the room began to echo with Elvis Presley crooning the sentimental ballad "Love Me Tender." The song reverberated with force off all four walls, making me dizzy. What was going on?

I was baffled for a solid moment but then realized Elvis was crooning the song the painter was listening to on his transistor radio the day he turned my bedroom bright yellow. Somehow the music was locked inside the wet paint and dried intact, stuck to my ceiling, waiting for this moment to come back to life.

I smelled fresh turpentine and burning electrical wires and looked around. The room was empty, and I got scared. Then I remembered what some famous physicist had said on TV years ago: "The universe is more like music than matter." Suddenly his words made sense. I put some of the crumbs of dried-up paint into my pocket for further study, and then I woke up.

 **MORE...**

Your home has its own sound signature. Even the seeming silence in each room sounds different. The way the coffeemaker gurgles sounds loud in the kitchen, but down the hall it is muffled and turns into a very mysterious underwater sound. This is not just hearing. It is active listening. Listen to the obvious hum of the refrigerator, the clacking clatter of the ice-maker, the sizzle of your lamp. It's easy to say the whirring of your heater is annoying or the buzzing of your computer obnoxious, but cut past the rating system of your brain, don't evaluate, and just listen.

What memories fill up the place? What words can you recall being spoken right at the front door? A good-bye? A poignant hello? What words were spoken in the living room? Do any sounds give you a sense of doom? Urgency? Joy? Expect the phone to ring? Is your washing machine shimmying across the room and driving you crazy? How about the cutting voice of your neighbor who's gabbing away right near your window? What's too loud? If you dare, turn on everything you can—the TVs, the radio, the blender—and experience the potential chaos and noise of just one house on the planet!

We rarely pay attention to everyday sounds unless something is wrong. The brain is designed that way. Some people live near train tracks or freeways. They get used to the continuous whooshing and rumble sound, day and night. But if some morning the freeway is shut down or the train doesn't come, it results in a very loud silence. Our brains wake us up from sound sleeps when something different happens, even if what happens is a loud nothing.

QUICK SNAP

20—SING "ROW, ROW, ROW YOUR BOAT"

Sing, "Row, Row, Row Your Boat Gently Down the Stream! Merrily, Merrily, Merrily, Merrily, Life Is But a Dream!" Too Many Times!

21—Vocalize the Vowels

Sing or yodel or chant the vowels A, E, I, O, U over
and over and over again. Relax as
the sounds fall out of your mouth.
Notice the skin on your face warming
up and your throat opening.

Tongue Work

I tried to learn German. It was tough. Especially the
vowels, sounds not found in English or any other language. I was always asking my teacher, "Where is your
tongue?" and "Should I pucker my lips?" I would ask,
"Is it *shoon* kinda like *moon*, or is it *shone*, more like
bone?" It's not just about learning how to make the
sounds, but when to make them. It gets subtle, kind of
like music, and fine precision makes the difference
between saying what you really mean and just forming
sounds.

I started watching a lot of German TV so I'd develop
more of an ear. One word I chose to practice a lot was
from a commercial selling fancy lamps. They compared
the light from a beautiful steel table lamp to the glow of
a single candle. This young woman would strike a
match and say, "Oh, streichholzschaechtelchen."

"Streich" means "to strike," and "holz" is "wood"—making the word "streichholz": "a match." "Schachtel" is "storage," and "-chen" is a suffix meaning "small and cute." So the gigantic, angled, choppy word "streich-holzschaechtelchen" means "a cute little box of matches."

I practiced that word over and over again until I got it right. There are four "ch"s in the word, which are usually murder for English-speakers. But I got it pretty easily, I think, because I watched the commercial over and over and froze the picture every time the young woman's tongue moved. Germans have the most amazing tongues and make the most amazing sounds.

MORE...

Singing is soothing and our voices seem to be designed to belt out a tune. Singing is massage from the inside out. Making sounds out loud opens up our throats, vibrates in our chests and bones, massages our hearts, and uplifts our spirits. Remember learning the vowels A, E, I, O, and U? Or did you learn them as A, E, I, O, U, and sometimes Y? A common teaching device was to teach the vowels as a song. Sing the letters out loud and run them together into a little hymn. It is a common warm-up exercise for professional singers. Singing "AaaaaEeeeeeIiiiiOooooUuuuuu" is hypnotic and turns into a kind of aural landscape.

Repeat the vowels over and over. Let the letters shift into beautiful sounds that allow your mouth to open and relax and your mind to melt. Try singing them loudly and then very softly for a few minutes. Then sit and listen to the echoes of the vowels resonating in your awareness and fading into silence. Toning, humming, or singing activates your brain. It wakes you up to the moment, alive and tuned in.

Sound is one of the main ways we receive and process the world. It shapes our lives, organizes our day, and offers us a sense of "ongoing-ness."

Sound literally means healthy, as in the phrase "of sound mind and body." Its roots come from "gesund," meaning legal, unbroken, thorough, and healthy. Sound also refers to being trustworthy and stable. We depend on the bells which toll the hours, and we rely on the buzz of the alarm to get us going. We respond to invasive sounds that don't sound "right," like footsteps or sirens or screams in the night.

The middle ear bones are the only bones in the body that are fully matured in size at birth. That means our auditory channels are ready from the get-go. Sound is profound. And the most vital piece of our acoustic environment is the human voice.

22—Wild Hoots

Make as many animal sounds
as you can. Growl and roar like
a wild cat in the jungle. Hoot,
holler, and whistle like exotic
birds in the tropics. Include sea
mammals, high-pitched dolphins, low-humming
whales. Open your teeth. Click, clack, and cackle.
Don't forget to include the domestic beasts in your
repertoire, like dogs and cows and chickens and pigs.

23—Shhhh...Whisper

Whisper one or more of the following: Peace, thank
you, I am, Amen, all is well, relax. Speak as softly as
possible while remaining audible. Get softer and
softer as you repeat your words of choice over and
over and over again.

Life's Perfect

I took a man I cared deeply about to an island for a vacation. I had waited for seven years, until the timing felt right. I dreamt about driving him to a special beach and together immersing ourselves in the warm turquoise waters. I treated him to the airfare and organized a detailed and romantic itinerary. At last we arrived at our destination and got into our rental car. I was excited with anticipation.

We drove to the nearest beach for a quick dip. As we entered the water things didn't feel quite right. The waves were larger than I expected, the air too still and humid, the sky too dark. He looked at me and smiled, saying, "Life's perfect."

I said, "No, it isn't. Something is off."

That night we heard an announcement on the radio. A big hurricane was possibly going to hit the island. We were advised to board up the house and stockpile some food. There might be a very long, very strong wind. But, the newscasters also suggested, the hurricane might bypass the island altogether. We knew that if we heard a loud siren blast in the early morning, Iniki was on her way.

At six o'clock in the morning a siren blew. Iniki ripped across the island for the next fourteen hours. The day after, we walked around the neighborhood to examine the damage. It was dramatic and devastating. We spent the next few days clearing up debris and helping other people make their homes more livable. Food and drinking water were scarce. Fortunately, we had squirreled away more than we needed and neighbors came by to help themselves.

Once the telephone poles were cleared out of the streets, we were free to drive around the area. I still had the dream of immersing with my male friend in the warm waters of the special beach. We made it to the end of the road and hiked to the trailhead that led down to it. I could see the outline of the rocks and the craggy cliffs as I peeked down, but there was a huge pole blocking the way. A large metal sign had recently been erected: "No Trespassing. Danger. Do Not Enter. Chocolate Water."

I couldn't believe it. Seven years of waiting and planning and now this. I leaned against the pole and tears welled up. I shook my head in deep disappointment. The winds suddenly picked up and I felt anxious. But my friend smiled at me with beaming eyes, gazed around the landscape, and whispered, "Life's perfect."

I mouthed the words back at him. "Life's perfect? "

He whispered even more softly. "Yes. Life's perfect."

 **MORE...**

When repeated over and over, words or special combinations of syllables are called *mantras*. Using a mantra entices the mind to go beyond its habitual noise and chatter. These words or syllables take you from the literal to the mystical. They are sacred ways of using your voice without necessarily having a religious overtone. Your voice becomes the gateway from the tangible to the the abstract. Giving voice builds a bridge between mind and body with breath as the vehicle. And whispering your mantra opens a pathway to a different kind of understanding. A whisper naturally soothes your mind while gently massaging your face and skull. A whisper is a subtle tool of breath and consciousness that creates calm and ease in the center of a storm.

24—Ear to the Ground

Put your ear against the wall, a door, the ground, a seashell, a clock, your kitten's belly. A great exploration is having someone put his or her mouth against your ear and then talk, hum, or gently whisper.

Snap, Crackle, and Pop

When I was a kid I usually gobbled a big bowl of cold milk, a mound of sugar, and Rice Krispies for breakfast. I'd bury my spoon in the sweet pile and then whip it into a fabulous pack of popping bubbles. Right before taking my last bite, I'd dunk my ear into the bottom of the chartreuse bowl, hold my breath, and listen. I swore I could hear the cereal talking. It was my first prepackaged oracle. Of course, I was never sure what it said, but I figured someone, somewhere could decode Rice Krispies and I'd simply have to grow up to find out.

 **MORE...**

Native Americans would literally put their ears to the ground to gather information about what was going on in their neighborhood. They could often distinguish the sounds of horse hoofs from various tribes from a distance of miles. We rarely put our ears to the ground, let alone bring anything up to our ears to examine what it sounds like. And rarely do our ears ever make contact with much more than an Ipod or Walkman earplug. We use our eyes and hands to discover the world. And, since everything is so loud now, we rarely need to listen closely. But get up close and personal. Check out what's really lurking in the acoustic bath that surrounds you. Learn to trust your ears.

25—DON'T BITE YOUR TONGUE

Speak whatever negative words, criticism, or nasty thoughts you have about yourself. Go on. Get it off your chest. Rage, rant, rave. Spout the words out loud. Don't forget to include all the things you were told so many times when you were growing up. Get carried away. Be melodramatic. Now, when you finish, take a breath and contradict all of those words. Say something nice about you.

True or False?

In the late sixties there was much turmoil and unrest in the world and on campus. To simplify things, the university chancellor designated one full year as the year without grades. You would simply pass or fail a class. I took Music Appreciation, a course that covered music from the first toot of the shofar in biblical times to contemporary rock and roll.

The final exam was rumored to be very difficult. We all crammed to the very last second. Finally it was test time. We took our seats in the huge music auditorium. The professor stepped on stage, opened the curtains, and sat down at an opaque projector. We shifted in our seats. "The final exam will not be handed out. I will write down the one question. You will see it projected up there, and then you will answer it. When you are done, drop your papers into this box." A teaching assistant wheeled in a gigantic United States mailbox that had been decorated a bright Day-Glo pink. The professor played pygmy music in the background and wrote the question in thick black grease pencil across the plastic sheet he projected onto the gigantic screen. The question was simply, "True or false?"

That was it? Yes. I didn't miss a beat. I answered the question, dropped my exam into the mailbox, and split for lunch. I later found out all the "True" answers received a pass and all the "False" answers received a fail. When I investigated further, I learned that only 25 percent of the class passed. I was one of them.

MORE...

Determining what is really true or false is not just the job of philosophers. All of us need to tune into our own true/false meter.

Words have great power. And words of criticism that hurt cannot be taken back. Even when they aren't true, if repeated enough times, they can become the seemingly impermeable building blocks of our self-esteem...or lack thereof. It takes time to undo what isn't true and label it as false. But it is possible. Speaking your own truth about yourself is powerful. Using your own voice and hearing yourself affirm your best literally gets under your skin and changes you on a profound level.

QUICK SNAP

26—COUNT OUT LOUD BACKWARD

Count Out Loud Backward from 100. Don't cheat. Don't Skip Any Numbers. Or...Belt Out "99 Bottles Of Beer On The Wall."

27—Bumblebee Buzz

Raise your hands to your face and bring your elbows to the level of your shoulders. Gently place your thumb tips in your ear holes to keep out external sounds. Use your index and middle fingers to lightly close your eyes. The middle fingertips draw the upper lids down and the index finger tips cover the remaining space above to keep out any light. Press your nostrils with your ring finger tips. It takes a little while to figure out. Let your hands relax and you'll find the link-up. Now keep your mouth closed and hum. Hum like a bumblebee until your whole head reverberates in a stimulating vibration.

Now change the vibration by opening up your lips, pushing your tongue lightly against your closed front teeth, and making a stronger, louder, vibratory buzzing sound. Stop after a few minutes. Listen. Notice a feeling of tranquility and inner sensual warmth wash over you.

Sounds of Silence and Cicadas

I drove four hours and fifteen minutes, parked my car, and walked about forty-five minutes down a winding trail. The air was crisp, the sky bright, and the Joshua trees barely moved in the stillness of the desert dusk. At last I lay down near an outcropping of red rocks and cacti. I closed my eyes. I stopped thinking. I stopped breathing, almost. And then it happened: I was caught in the silence. It gripped me, almost hurting me as I felt squeezed between the sounds of nothing. It was exquisite, a place of hidden beauty. I swallowed and the whooshing and rumblings inside my body filled my head with a rumble.

Ten years earlier I had flown fifteen hours and driven another fifty to a remote park in New Zealand. I walked down a narrow flagstone path to an outcropping of exotic-looking sunlit trees. No one was around. I stopped walking. I lay down. I closed my eyes. I stopped thinking. And then it happened: I was bombarded by a deafening cacophony of noise. It was a chorus of male cicadas screaming out what are loosely called songs by using a pair of ridged membranes found on their abdomens, which are hollow and act as resonating chambers. Females do not sing, but with a quick flip of their wings, create a broad frequency that sounds like a sharp pop. It was like an invisible onslaught of ten thousand freight trains carrying ten thousand high school marching bands. My ears vibrated out of control from wild shrieking alarm calls and rough and staccato buzzes. I finally understood the story from Bible class about Joshua fighting the battle of Jericho. I never believed noise could be so powerful, but after hearing these cicadas, I could see how those soldiers' endless blasting of noisy, deafening horns could have set up the ultimate unbearable frequency to make those walls come tumbling down!

I found myself running as fast as I could out of that remote sanctuary. I covered my ears and kept moving. And then something happened: There was this huge silent gap that caught me by surprise, hitting my body full force from the outside in, the way a football linebacker might when he comes right at you. I found myself on my back, rolling into a tree, wondering what had happened.

MORE...

Humming is a very intimate form of creating and feeling your inner warmth. It is a quick way to surround yourself with yourself. Keep the tune or buzz going over and over until it vibrates down into your bones. Bones are moist and resilient, and sound can penetrate them. Deaf people standing next to a large sound speaker can feel the vibration and a bath of energy in their bones. This primal feeling recreates the pulse and rhythm of being next to your mother's heart or floating in the womb.

When you stop humming, recognize the silence and understand that silence is not the same as soundlessness. Listen into silence. It can be sullen or hostile. Hot, heavy, prickly. Time stands still and impales the listener. Other silences are warm, enveloping, nurturing.

28—Who Am I?

Repeat "Who am I?" over and over and over and over. Take a full two minutes. Get still and ask, "What do I do now?" Listen. Trust the you that answers the question.

MORE...

Reality is layered, like an onion. Asking questions is one of the ways you can peel off the layers one by one, to find out what is real for you, now. It is also a way to develop an intimate relationship with yourself.

Asking, "Who am I?" will desolidify your identity. For a split second, you may feel your-self leave your body only to return to make a new connection. Asking, "What do I do now?" gives you a tool for cultivating your intuition. Learning to listen for the answer is a skill that brings great rewards. Questioning draws out your truth. Revelation is in the process. Never trade a good question for an answer! Keep asking. Keep listening.

29—The I Am List

Make a list of apparent answers to the question "Who am I?" Swing the other direction and this time, list aloud as many solid identities as you can. Start each sentence with, "I am..."

My name

I am how old?

My relationship identities (I am a mother, wife, boss, etc.)

My official job titles

Educational degrees

Hobbies

Secrets (arrest, drug record)

My religious identity

My political identity

My ethnic identity

My sexual identity

My marital status history

My children's names and ages

My possession identities

The clubs

Ma's Accent

I received a reel-to-reel tape recorder for my thirteenth birthday. I decided to hide it underneath the dining room table to audiotape dinner. My mother, father, sister, brother, and grandmother gathered around for brisket and potatoes. We ate, talked, argued, whined, blamed, laughed, and told jokes—the usual. After dinner I sat everyone down in the den and played what I had recorded. We all were amused and a little surprised at how boring we were. But my grandmother sat erect and riveted to the machine. She got closer and closer to listen better. At last she asked, "Who's the lady with the accent? I am not that woman." My grandmother was from Russia and had a thick accent. "That's

you, Ma," I smiled. She shook her head in disbelief.
She never knew she had an accent until then.

   **MORE...**

The voice is an important part of our sense of being.
It defines and expresses our personality. "I don't
sound like that," is the response most people make as
they listen to a recording of their own voice. It frus-
trates and confuses. Why do we sound like someone
else? It's odd how such a schism can exist between
what we hear in our heads and what the world identi-
fies as us. But listening to ourselves is much more
complex than identifying a sound. It is identifying a
living, breathing organism whose sound vibrations
have been captured in metal. Who is that person?
How inscrutable are we?

Uncertainty is what makes life rich. The mystery of
who we are will continue, no matter how many pho-
tographs, voice recordings, videos, or lengthy lists of
"Who Am I" we gather. Mastery and self-knowledge
is what we strive for, but mystery is what we are left
with. So court the mystery and be surprised. Ask,
"Who am I?" but don't get caught up in the answers.

30—CLICK YOUR TEETH

*Lightly Click Your Teeth Together
for One Full Minute*

31—LEND AN EAR

Ask yourself the following four big questions. First
state them out loud. Then hear them silently inside
your head. Close your eyes if it helps you to answer
more honestly.

Am I hungry now?   **Am I angry now?**

Am I lonesome now?   **Am I tired now?**

 MORE...

Sometimes we feel out of sorts or stuck in a mental
loop and we begin to worry. We fret. We get anxious.
We might even panic. Although there could be some
underlying causes that are creating this emotional
disturbance, it is often wise to ask the four big questions first, to clarify the situation. When we were kids,
we may have had a raging temper tantrum only to
realize what we really needed was a peanut butter
and jelly sandwich. Find out if you are hungry, angry,

lonesome, or tired. Be gentle and honest with yourself and then take good care. Have a snack. Identify your anger and spout it out. Call a friend. Take a nap. Usually food, expression, contact, and rest handle even the most difficult times.

32—MOUTH TRICKS

Pretend you are swishing mouthwash around in your mouth hard and fast. Now lick your lips and do whatever mouth tricks you remember from childhood. Stick your finger in your cheek and mimic the sound of a champagne bottle popping open. Make all the "disgusting" sounds you weren't supposed to make but did. Roll your rrrrr's. Spit. Even swear a little.

 MORE...

It seemed that when boys reached the fifth grade, they discovered how to generate hideous mouth sounds. While most girls learned to giggle and stay out of trouble, the boys concocted elaborate, ear-popping, over-the-top whistles and gurgles, belches, snorts, and something else that took place under their armpits, resulting in a loud alien suction snap. Although the result for these brave clowns was a slow stroll to the principal's office, the rest of us reaped the rewards of a warm, stimulating, spasmodic, rhythmic, vocalized, expiratory expulsion of air. Human laughter.

33—KISS KISS

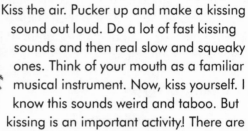

Kiss the air. Pucker up and make a kissing sound out loud. Do a lot of fast kissing sounds and then real slow and squeaky ones. Think of your mouth as a familiar musical instrument. Now, kiss yourself. I know this sounds weird and taboo. But kissing is an important activity! There are things you can learn about kissing only by experimenting on yourself first. Try your forearm. Start with brushing your lips just above the skin, so that you are touching only the hairs. Listen to the brushing sound. There are at least two areas to listen to—your lips and the area of your forearm. After you get used to very light kisses, give your forearm a big, wet, noisy kiss.

Reddi-Whip

As a child, I loved Oreos. Who wouldn't? Those crispy chocolate wafers filled with a perfect circle of sugar were totally irresistible. But to make them even better, my brother and I would add a loud, delicious squirt of whipped cream. Our neighbor, Mr. Lipsky, had just invented Reddi-Whip. He had lived through World War II and had dreamed it up when he was stuck on the front lines somewhere in Luxembourg.

I'd shake the pressurized can, which looked just like a rocket ship, until I could barely breathe, then snap off its bright red top and squirt out dollops of white cream on cookie after cookie. My favorite thing was to decorate my arms and my brother's with long white wiggles. Then we'd suck up the stuff with amazing speed and do it again and again. My brother was really adventurous. When mom was off on errands, he'd skip the cookies altogether and squirt the contents of the canister right into his mouth!

One day Mr. Lipsky came by. He got a kick out of watching us go crazy with his new device. Then he showed us something special. He pushed very slowly on the little plastic lever, and, with great finesse, decorated our arms with a dozen perfect little flowerets. "Instead of acting like little vacuum cleaners," he said, "how about kissing those white delights until they melt in your mouth and disappear?" Lipsky whispered, "Whipped cream is meant to be kissed."

I thought he was being weird, but Lipsky was a well-known scientist—maybe this was research for an important new invention, so I figured, why not? There we were, right in the middle of our pink and green breakfast nook, making the weirdest sounds ever as we puckered up our lips while Mr. Lipsky (who later struck it rich as the creator of Gravy Train for dogs) hooted, hollered, and egged us on!

 **MORE...**

Kissing is both giving and receiving. Your lips feel the warmth coming off the skin, plus some of your breath will bounce off the skin and create sensations around the nostrils. It also smells, tastes, and sounds good. It creates a subtle sound, a sound very fundamental to being human. If you listen when you kiss softly you'll hear how it mimics birds clattering, dogs licking their lips, cats preening, and fish making soft bubbling sounds underwater.

Explore kissing a little. Have you ever kissed your pillow? You don't need to get carried away, just a few light kisses will do. This is not an experiment in self-arousal. This is an exploration into subtle sound sensation and self-knowledge. Kiss your hands, your fingers, your feet if you can. Acknowledge each part of your body as a wonder of nature, a special place for giving and receiving, a musical instrument.

34—SOUNDS IN THE NIGHT

Listen to the sounds in the night. Just stick your head out the back door or crack open a window. If you dare, slide outside and hunker down. What do you hear? The wind rustling? Dogs barking? A train? Neighbors fighting? A distant fire engine? Helicopters chasing a burglar? Soak it all in. Take enough time to cut through

the debris and stuff that normally drives you nuts.
Notice what's going on below the obvious. Animals
scurrying? Birds softly chirping? Your heart beating?

 MORE...

It's getting harder and harder to find darkness or
silence. Our lives are faster, brighter, and louder than
ever. But no matter the noise or light pollution, night-
time is still the best time for listening. It has a sound
quality all its own. Without the deafening drone of the
lawn mower or leaf blower, our ears get to take a
break. Alone at night, new sounds show up and
familiar sounds may become even larger or more
daunting. Our ears perk up and sounds seem to leap
out at us. They seem physical, as the hair on our
neck stands up in anticipation. Is that the screen
door? Or a burglar? Was that the swing? Or a monster? No matter our age, sounds at night brew a
scary visceral stew.

As you listen longer, you will distinguish something
beyond the chatter of your mind and the residue of
your busy day. Like an engineer in an audio mixing
booth, we have the ability to move some sounds to
the rear and bring others up front. Even in loud urban
areas, you'll quickly cut through your neighbor's TV
and honking horns and absorb the clicking of a
nearby grasshopper, the hooting of an owl, or the

scurrying of a possum. A distant foghorn may enter your sphere, or an echo you know but can't identify.

All kinds of vivid sensations percolate into our hearts and minds when we linger in the night. There's something raw and primitive about it. Remember sitting around a campfire and hearing things that went bump? Get bumped again. Let the sounds of night wash over you, seep into your ears, and jar you awake. You may be surprised at how this experience uncovers memories and insights you've forgotten. Then, when you are ready, slip back into bed, turn on your soothing sound machine, and choose a favorite prepackaged loop. What's tonight? Rain? An aviary? Waterfalls, surf, ebb tide, or a steam train? Good night.

35—HEAR NO EVIL

Take your ears in your hands and gently massage the tops and bottoms until they warm up. Then curl each ear together like a little seashell connecting top and bottom. Allow them to open again and this time cover

each ear lightly with the palms of your hands. This move helps you tune out distracting noises and tune in to more intimate body rhythms and sounds. Create a bit of suction and simply listen. What do you hear? What don't you hear?

MORE...

You probably recognize this familiar gesture. It mirrors Mikazaru, one of the three Wise Monkeys from Japan who covered his ears so he would hear no evil. He's joined by his two other monkey pals, one who sees no evil, the other who speaks no evil. They illustrate a seventh century proverb stating that if we do not hear, see, or speak evil, we ourselves shall be spared evil.

Many of us spent a good part of our childhood just naturally covering up our ears to inform our siblings or parents we didn't want to listen. Sometimes we'd hum loudly too. Don't talk to me! I'm not here! Leave me alone! This protective posture has other subtle benefits. The fingers wrap around an area of the front of the head and temples that soothes the mind and relaxes the jaw. It's a quick way to calm down and refocus.

QUICK SNAP

36—POUND YOUR FISTS ON YOUR CHEST

Pound Your Fists on Your Chest and Do an Ear-Popping Tarzan Call of the Wild

37—STOP MAKING SENSE

Sit or stand or pace. Speak nonsense. That's right. Go the obvious "Blah, blah, blah" route. Or maybe "Yada, Yada, Yada." Speak in tongues, gobbledygook, baby talk, or pretend you know Russian and spout a loud speech. How about crooning a question over and over to a familiar tune? Try singing, "What am I doing now-ow, What am I doing now-ow, What am I doing now-ow; I have no idea" to the music for "We Wish You A Merry Christmas."

 **MORE...**

Nonsense frees us up. It helps us drop our assumptions about what's true and shatters a stiff moment of seriousness and the mental limitations that come from too much logic. By busting out of the expected, nonsense allows us to see new patterns. Remember how much fun it felt to open our imagination as we read a string of words that just didn't make any sense spoken by the walrus in *Alice In Wonderland*? "The time has come to think of many things: of shoes and ships and sealing wax, of cabbages and kings, of why the sea is boiling hot and whether pigs have wings."

Combining unusual words and ideas breaks the rules and cuts through habits fast. Choose something from a book or movie if you can't make something up yourself. If you're stuck, try the famous words from the sci-fi movie *The Day the Earth Stood Still*: "Klaatu Barada Nikto." It works for me every time.

CHAPTER 3

The
Eyes
Have
It

38—INFINITY EYES

Lift your right thumb up, pointing to the ceiling, in front of your face, and gaze at it with both eyes. You resemble the classic painter, holding his thumb out as he studies his subject. Now, watch your right thumb as it moves up to the right and trace an imaginary infinity sign. If you don't know what that looks like, imagine a figure eight lying on its side.

Keep your head still and your thumb at eye level. Follow the shape and create a nice flow, repeating it over and over. Now use your other thumb, making sure you start the shape by going up to the right. Finally, clasp both hands and outline infinity with hands together.

 MORE...

The symbol of an eight on its side is known as the lemniscate, which means "ribbon" in Latin. Most of us are familiar with it from math class as the symbol for infinity. The Magician, the first card in the Tarot, is often depicted with the lemniscate floating above his head or incorporated into a wide-brimmed hat, signifying the divine forces he is attempting to control.

Infinity Eyes doesn't guarantee divine powers, but it does strengthen your eye muscles so that you have more access to your peripheral vision. It also integrates the right and left visual fields of the brain, increasing balance and coordination.

The figure eight configuration is also a very basic shape that mirrors how we propel ourselves through space. It reflects the alternating wave between convexity and concavity, and is core to the way we organize our movements. We may not be aware of it, but we often trace a figure eight as we walk, wiggle, or crawl. On a deep level we all identify with this basic shape depicting the profound cyclic harmony we have known since the dawn of life.

39—Old-Time Movie

Blink your eyes really fast. Open, close, open, close. Create the effect of watching an old-time movie. Now squeeze your eyes tightly shut for a moment. Open your eyes and do another round of quick blinking.
Close your eyes tightly one more time, and then relax.

 MORE...

Rapid blinking stimulates your tear ducts and bathes your eyes with more tears than usual. This natural moisture is therapeutic and cleansing for the eyes. It is a great time to enjoy the pleasure of simply keeping your eyes gently closed. Notice how your eye sockets and the muscles and skin around the eyes feel.

Simply witness these marvelous windows to the other world with the shades drawn.

Flickering Eyes

Mona Lisa's smile has made us wonder for the last five hundred years. We look at da Vinci's masterpiece and see she is smiling. Then the smile fades. Then it reappears. What's with this lady's face? "Sfumato" is the word Italians have used to explain Mona Lisa's smile. It means blurry, ambiguous, and up to the imagination. But current science has a more specific explanation. Mona Lisa's smile comes and goes, not because her expression is ambiguous, but because of how the human visual system is designed.

The human eye has two distinct regions for seeing the world—the central area where people see colors, read fine print, and pick out details, and the peripheral area where people see black and white, motion, and shadows. Whenever we look at anything, our eyes and brain deal with a constant processing of light and its different levels of contrast and illumination.

When you stare at the Mona Lisa, you may notice a kind of flickering quality. The smile seems to come and go as a function of where your eyes are as you look at her. When you look at a face, your eyes usually focus on the other person's eyes. So, when your gaze is on Mona Lisa's eyes, your less accurate peripheral vision is on her mouth. And because peripheral vision is not interested in detail, it readily picks up shadows from Mona Lisa's cheekbones. These shadows suggest and enhance the curvature of a smile.

But when your eyes go directly to Mona Lisa's mouth, your central vision does not see the shadows. You just cannot catch her smile by looking at her mouth! The flickering quality—smile present, smile gone—occurs as you move your eyes around Mona Lisa's face. So, to make a good counterfeit Mona Lisa, you would have to paint the mouth by looking away from it. How anyone can do that still remains a mystery.

40—MORE THAN MEETS THE EYE

Stop whatever you are doing and look all around you. Notice the drapes, carpet, antique vase, pile of papers, stamps, glasses, even dust bunnies. Let your eyes settle on an object nearby. Maybe it's a book or a photograph. Take one long, luxurious, fully-dilated look. Notice the patterns, textures, shapes, colors, and beauty in this everyday object. Look at it as though you have never seen it before.

Now focus on two things nearby. Maybe the horse statue in the corner and your steaming cup of tea on the desk. Build a visual relationship between them. Consider their similarities and differences.

Mitochondria and the Paisley Dress

I spent hours gazing at tiny creatures under my microscope. The pond in the backyard provided me with some very interesting specimens. The creatures seemed so out of place in my world. I watched them like I watched people on TV, confused a bit about their size and where they came from.

One day my sister came over and took a peek. "Oh that's a cute paramecium," she exclaimed as she squinted into the eyepiece.

"Which one?"

"The one that looks like a ballet slipper."

I couldn't figure out which one she meant. You can't point to things under a microscope. Your fingers are too big. She peeked again.

"The creatures that look just like the paisley on your dress are the paramecia."

I squinted into the eyepiece and looked hard at my dress and she was right. It looked like it was covered with hundreds of paramecia. I wondered if the designer of the material looked into a microscope for inspiration. Suddenly I felt connected to the universe. My dress matched a creature of nature. Tears came to my eyes and life seemed real.

MORE...

Our eyes give us one way of touching the world and in turn, we feel touched by what we see. They also put divergent objects into one shared visual frame. Suddenly everything ties together in the direction of our gaze. When we pay attention, the objects begin to tell their stories and everything becomes more interesting. Observation breeds intimacy. We see colors and shapes we never knew existed. Look at your water glass, fountain pen, or even computer mouse. Enjoy how this seemingly ordinary thing oozes meaning, calls up memories, and delights.

Our eyes, when given the opportunity, peel off the layers, and details reveal themselves. The vague pattern on the couch becomes a code. The shape of a reading lamp becomes a female form. We choose things in our homes to give us pleasure and then we often forget to take a second look. Give yourself permission to let your gaze linger up close and personal on all of the objects that make up your life.

Basking in the details also changes our relationship with time itself. Time slows down when we enter into the rich texture of reality.

Our eyes are the great monopolists of our senses. They allow us to gaze, to study, to observe, to witness, to soak it all in. 70 percent of the body's sense receptors cluster in the eyes, and it is mainly through seeing the world that we size it up and understand it. Yet there is much more to seeing than plain seeing. One image can trigger thousands of responses because each individual perceives in a very personal way.

41—Eagle Eye

Look out the window. Now look beyond where your eyes normally land. If they latch onto the neighbor's telephone pole, pick them up and push them past. Pretend you are a bird of prey and feel how you might consciously scan the distance to connect with something that piques your interest. How about that tall chimney down the road? Or maybe zoom into the edge of the hillside. If possible, stretch your gaze and let your eyes touch the horizon. Hang out in the outer limits of your sight zone.

Clouds on Vacation

I injured my back and went on a little vacation to take a break. I rented a cabin and brought along a bunch of pillows and a stack of books. I was in a lot of pain and just figured I'd lie around and hide out. I sat down on the little porch, closed my eyes, and tried not to feel too sorry for myself. A loud rustle startled me and I opened my eyes to catch a glimpse of a brown hawk circling overhead.

As I gazed out, I realized I was facing a huge expanse of empty space, filled only with distant mountain peaks and thousands of fluffy white clouds. They looked like they were moving in super fast motion across the bluest of skies. I opened my eyes wider to take it all in, and I felt as though I had fallen into another dimension.

There were so many of these clouds, all white and fluffy, changing shape rapidly from moment to moment. I watched them dance and spin and parade. My initial reaction was to say, "Enough," and get up to go. But the truth was, I had nowhere to go and nothing else to do. So I decided to commit to watching one single cloud make its way across my entire field of vision. I chose a fat ball that looked like a coconut which shifted almost instantly into a couple of dolphins cutting through water, which turned into a pair of nasty gargoyles, into two lovers melting together, into a sudden flurry of tiny pieces of Kleenex, which dissolved into nothing just like that! I spent at least five hours the first day watching as these mysterious semimaterial objects were born, changed shape, cast shadows, and disappeared.

After a while, my eyes began to tear and ache. Maybe I wasn't blinking enough, I don't know, but I was still mesmerized. Sometimes I noticed I lost the cloud I had my eye on because I was looking way too hard at it. I remembered the astronomical axiom that in order to really see a constellation you couldn't look right at it but had to soften your gaze and look just to the side. When I went to Australia to see Halley's Comet the same rule held. Only when I was willing to scan the sky gently, without trying too hard, did the Q-Tipped blur of a comet come into view.

When I finally went inside for a sandwich I felt disoriented, the way you feel when you come out of a movie theater in the middle of the afternoon. But as time went by, I found myself growing a new set of eyes. I had been transported into another world and was learning how to navigate with my eyeballs.

The last day of my vacation it rained. I sat inside for the very first time, and instead of looking way out there I turned my vision up close in here. I started off gazing at a bowl of steaming chicken noodle soup. What a discovery! It seems once your eyes are open, the mystery

and beauty of life can serenade you, no matter where
you are or what you are doing.

MORE...

You can't see what's behind you by looking twice as
hard at what's in front of you. Moving your focus
from right in front to up, down, and then the full 360
degrees opens you up to new visions and new ideas.
But most of us are so absentminded. Our scattershot
attention is rarely focused, let alone expansive. Taking
the time to look out our picture windows brings so
many simple surprises.

Our lives are graced with natural beauty. Even a leaf,
dried and crumpled, upon closer scrutiny reveals an
entire universe. Allow your eyes to leap up and out of
your comfort zone. Our eyes love novelty, but we can
never truly say we have seen the moon and are done
with her. And moonlight itself is so magical. It lights
up our faces as it creates shadows of mystery along
the familiar terrain of our own neighborhood streets.
Soften your gaze and look at the moon. Now take the
index finger of your dominant hand and point. We
rarely point, but it is a powerful act. It builds a clear
sight line between head and heart, like holding a bow
in hand and aiming. Stand tall. Point, but don't mistake your index finger for the moon!

QUICK SNAP

42—GAZE AT YOUR NAVEL

43—Things Unseen

Stare at a shadow cast against the wall from the sun or a reflection that comes from a light source inside your home. It is not easy focusing on a soft, disem-

bodied shape. Keep your focus and notice what happens to your eyes and your mind. Where does this shadow really exist? Where does the object begin and the shadow of the object end?

Reflections on a Sun Hat

The late summer sunlight shines through the window onto my old sun hat hanging on a peg next to the front door. The sycamore leaves across the street cast a moving shadow that plays across the woven yellow surface. My eyes automatically try to focus on the flickering shapes that dance in the middle of the hat. But it's almost impossible. Some things are meant to melt in your mouth. Others melt in your eyes. The more I stare the harder it is. Like a battle between reason and dreams. This is not a clear picture and it feels freeing, to gaze softly and let this gentle experience wash over me. I feel like I've slipped through a rip in my life and have suddenly been given permission to hover in the pure...what is it...yes, beauty of a sun hat hanging on a wall. I bet this thing happens every day in my den, but it has never caught me until now.

I admit I see no Virgin Mary. No baby Jesus. No DNA. A simple moment of...but wait...it's changing again. The Earth has slipped a little and the shadow play is different. Now I see Camille's face shaking her head "No." She is there but gone and now I see a sad-eyed clown, then my Aunt Anita with a cigarette, then the outline of a cowboy boot. It never stops shifting. I think I'll stay and wait it out.

This feeling reminds me of being a child, playing outside in the lingering summer nights, part of the deliciously slow fade to black. And like clockwork, the minute I delighted in the feeling of being out alone my mom would call me in to dinner. I stand up to get a closer look, but the magic is gone. And for now, it is just my hat again, hanging innocently enough, on a peg near the door.

MORE...

There are certain moments in the day when the sun's light casts a glow that begs you to stop, slow down, and reflect. Morning light has a gentle radiance and with it comes a sense of freshness and clarity. Noon shadows are crisp, and at dusk, when the polarities of the day and night meet, the sky puts on a show of dazzling color. These moments prompt us to take a breather and recognize that there is, in nature, a force that is capable of showering us with beauty and bringing joy if we just take a peek and let it.

44—EYELID LIGHT SHOW

Close your eyes and turn your face to a bright light. You can move to the window and let the sun dance across your eyelids or aim your face at a brightly-lit lamp. As you keep your eyes closed, be aware of what you see on the inside of your eyelids. Rub your eyes gently and now what appears? Are there colors? Shapes?

Brain Waves

I read about brain waves and I thought that if people have these electrical impulses in their brains, you could just pick them up and feed them into a TV set. You could see what they were thinking, what they were dreaming, and the pictures in their heads. So I got some dimes, which in 1960 were made out of pure silver, and I hammered them into an electrode paste. Then I hooked up my friend by putting these electrodes on his temples (he was eight, I was ten). I connected the electrodes to the antennae input of the big old Dumont TV set the size of a modern refrigerator and a screen about eight inches diagonal.

I tuned it to channel two. Blank. Channel thirteen was blank, too. I tried all the blank stations. We saw nothing. No thoughts, no dreams, no pictures from his head. I figured the set-up needed more oomph so I hooked him, a 10,000-volt spark coil, and the antennae inputs of the TV together. Of course, he jumped six feet and ran home to his mom. It blew out the TV and I got grounded.

MORE...

The slight pressure of your eyelids on your cornea and
the tiny flickering of your eye muscles produce mini-
hallucinations called entropic lights. They are definitely
something to look at. Also called "dark noise," they
change their shape and color when you rub your eyes.
They flower into a psychedelic palette and shimmer
with mysterious auroras, ghosts, and designs.

Most of us remember playing all kinds of optical illusion games when we were young. One of the classic
eye tricks from childhood was looking at a particular
black and white image and being asked, "Do you see
the young lady or the old woman?" Another familiar
trick was viewing the image of two profiles or one
large vase and wondering, "What do you see? A vase
or two faces?" Staring a while changes everything.

 SNAP TO YOUR IMAGINATION

45—I CAN SEE FOR MILES AND MILES

Pretend you are a mountain. Your legs are made out
of granite, strong and solid. Your head reaches the
heavens and cuts through the cloud cover. From this

 vantage point you can look out in 360
degrees along the horizon line of the
planet. Gaze at the vast vistas. You are
solid.

46—ARE YOU BLUE?

Look for something in your home that is the color blue. Now take a few moments and with a soft gaze, allow the color blue to seep into your eyes and being. Notice the object's shape and outline and design. Can you get inside the outline and just melt into the color field? Blue is considered the most popular color. How does it make you feel?

 **MORE...**

We are born into this world in living color. Our skin glows brown, peach, olive, and yellow. Our hair sparkles platinum, black, and auburn. The iris of the eye, named after the Greek word for rainbow, is what gives our eyes their color. Color doesn't appear in the world. It appears in our eyes. We interpret light. Each wavelength of color is a different architectural wavelength on a microscopic scale. These wavelengths are really scattered light rays that bounce back and are interpreted by our brain. Illusion is at the heart of color. Traced back to its Indo-European root "kel," color means to "hide." Color is hidden from human view and then retrieved by the educated and inspired eye.

Many of our very first memories are seeped in color. Profound, unforgettable impressions: The red ball. The yellow blanket. The purple flower. Color gripped us from the start and continues to thrill us with its power, charm, and magic. It saturates our emotions, moods, and thoughts. The impact of the first time we pricked our finger and saw the rich redness of our insides, stood in awe of a vibrant orange sunset, or were blinded by the whiteness of the blasting full moon touches our very souls; and in many ways, our souls are multifaceted expressions of pure color at its finest.

47—Things That Crawl

Stop what you are doing. Look around. Look up, look down. Allow your eyes to settle on the ground, the floor, and the carpet. Where else can you look? How about under the rug? Look for things that crawl, or at least places where things could crawl. Look under your desk, the couch, and your bed. Literally look in the places you have been avoiding. It could be the back of the closet or the bottom drawer in the pantry. This isn't about cleaning house or killing insects. It is about opening your eyes to the ground floor of your world. What have you been avoiding? Notice the surprises you find. Any apprehension? Come on now. Get on your knees.

Expansiveness

I noticed a slip of white paper stuck under my plastic garbage can. It looked like a business card. I didn't feel like bending over to pick it up, so I left it there for a few days. By garbage day it was getting pretty shredded and funky so I figured I should throw it out. I reached down and just as I was about to toss it, I took a closer look. It was really dirty on one side. But when I turned it over, written across the middle in large block letters was just one word: Expansiveness.

I laughed out loud. Aha! Was I being given some important information? My logical mind tried to place the reference. I had recently purchased a backpack and figured this must be part of the advertising junk I pulled out and tossed. But whether it was marketing hype or a major Zen koan, expansiveness was hiding under my garbage can, waiting for me to take a peek.

The irony wasn't wasted. I decided to take the cue. I opened my arms, took a big breath, and sighed. As I leaned back I noticed a blue jay's nest snuggled into my back door awning. Then I saw a tiny lavender viola popping out of a plant that had taken root between the tiles on the roof. A pair of crows was watching all of this and cawed loudly. A cloud floated by that resembled a dog I used to have. The moon was rising in a beautiful circle of fog. Venus showed up in the dusk sky and then my neighbor turned on a Beethoven symphony.

It pays to bend over, pay attention, and be expansive. I couldn't believe this momentary glimpse of what I guess happens every evening, right next to my plastic garbage can.

48—Xxxcellent X

With your eyes wide open, draw the letter X at eye level with your finger. Follow the movement of your finger with your eyes as it goes up and down and to the sides. Do this two or three times.

Now close your eyes and visualize a large X. See the center of the X and let the edges fade away. With eyes closed, keep moving them under your eyelids tracing the letter over and over again. Then, let your eyes come to rest in the middle. Allow yourself to become interested in the intersection of the lines and say the sound "X" to yourself a few times.

If you do not see the letter X in your mind's eye, explore drawing it on a piece of paper in a big, bold gesture. The motion your arms make when drawing will help your body to attune to the meaning and shape of X. When you have made an X that you like, look at it and trace the shape of the letter with your eyes. Then close your eyes and see the letter, and again move your eyes along the lines toward the intersection.

Xxxcellent Story

I'll never forget that first day of algebra. Mrs. Alba Khowaraizmi drew one huge white X right in the middle of the blackboard, smiled knowingly, and announced, "Class, this year it's all about X." Wow. What happened to numbers? Mrs. Khowaraizmi, a distant relative of the Arab mathematician from Baghdad who apparently gave algebra its name, was truly over the top. She shouted out formulas, screeched exponential factors, and even demanded that right before we went to sleep we needed to always consider the value of the unknown.

I liked the look of the letter X and came to appreciate that it could stand for anything. From its ancient pictographic symbolism for a wooden post (the kind of thing that held up a house or eliminated a vampire), X grew to encompass all kinds of possibilities. "Let X equal..." was the daily mantra, and although algebra proved a tad too mysterious for me, it also revealed the deeply profound relationship between symbols and what we decide they mean.

To make sure we got it, Mrs. Khowaraizmi had us part-ner up. I was stuck with little Eddie Parker. When the teacher shouted "X marks the spot!" he drew with his pudgy index finger an invisible giant X from shoulder to hip on both sides of my pink shirtmaker dress. Then we switched, and I did it on Eddie's faded overalls. It was weird how something so abstract could feel so good, solid, and real.

 MORE...

Open your eyes and notice how you feel. Do you feel just a tiny bit more centered? Do you have a slight sense of relaxation? Doing Xxxcellent X for even thirty seconds can be powerful. The movements your eyes make when following the X are comprehensive— down to the left, up to the right, down to the right, up to the left. It's good exercise for the eyes and the brain. It also allows your brain to cross the midline of the body, with the eyes as the guide, which connects the right and left visual fields, both sides of the body for coordinated movement, and both hemispheres of the brain for integrative thinking.

For extra credit, notice people's eye movements when they are talking in ordinary conversation. Sometimes they move their eyes to the left or right, up to the right or left, or down to the left or right. Everyone is differ-ent, but there is some correlation with people moving their eyes up when they are thinking in pictures, down when they are having a feeling, and to the left or right when they are thinking in words.

49—SEE NO EVIL

Rub your hands together rapidly and create some heat. Now cup them over your eyes, right palm on right eye, left on left. Do not rest on the eyeballs directly. Only put pressure around the eye socket. Gently cover your eyes so that you do not see any light. Keep your eyes open and gaze into the darkness or gently close your eyes. The duration is up to you. It can be as short as ten seconds or up to a few minutes. Absorb the warmth and rest.

Electricity

Elementary school auditorium. A red velvet curtain. A large silver ball balances on top of a black wooden podium. A man in a white lab coat steps up onto the stage. Temi Millstein, the girl with the longest hair in all eight grades, walks up and shakes hands with the guest scientist. He gazes out at all of us waiting in the dark and then turns to Temi. "When I say, 'Now,' I want you to reach out your left hand and place it on top of that large silver ball, ever so lightly." The lights go down. "Now," the scientist whispers.

Temi reaches out and touches the shiny ball. Instantly, her waist-length hair flies into the air in all directions, like some seductive sea creature floating in a body of warm water. A soft sizzle whistles across the auditorium. My ears vibrate. "Electricity," the scientist announces. "Our silent servant." I gasp. Something mysterious seems to be crawling up and down my spine.

 *MORE...*

Eye palming is an ancient technique that provides relief for tired or dry eyes and promotes deep relaxation. It also creates a mini-electrical field that stimulates your skin and nerve endings. And it is visually stimulating as well. In the darkness, you may see brief flashes of light. This is normal and simply indicates the spontaneous firing of the neurons in your eyes. But if the light flashes are too intense, they may indicate that you are too tense. Loosen up a bit! Nobody's watching you.

50—Upside Down

Bend over. Look at the world upside down. As you hang over, imagine that along your spinal column all the vertebrae make a long rope of knots. Now bring awareness to these knots and with the weight of your head, allow gravity to unravel them one by one. Get longer. Surrender to the force. Feel its pull and give in.

Earthrise

It was Christmas Eve, 1968. A year of tumultuous political chaos and teenage confusion. I was parked up on a hill overlooking the glistening city lights, listening to the flight report on my boyfriend's car radio. Apollo 8 was actually up there, somewhere, with three astronauts on board. But the news guy said the moon was invisible, hidden in shadow, lost in total darkness.

One of the things that would tell the astronauts whether they were on track was a certain point in the flight plan when they were to look down and see the sunrise impacting the lunar surface. At the exact second they were supposed to see it, something else caught their eyes. The rough lunar mountains on the dark side of the moon were revealed! And then something else happened that no one expected. The astronauts looked up and saw a very fragile ball of blue coming up on the moon's horizon—the Earth—floating all alone in the blackness of space.

I was blinded by huge searchlights from some noisy helicopter, probably tracking a burglar, and could hear the loud music blasting out of a few neighboring cars' eight tracks. As I tuned into the news I felt overcome with the magnitude of what I was hearing. These three guys had gone all this way to photograph the moon, but the most significant thing they got to see and freeze on film was the Earth. This was a lesson in perspective. Here we were, battling it out over differences that seemed so irreconcilable. North and South Vietnam. Men and women. Arab and Jew. (When the unforgettable photograph called "Earthrise" came out in poster form, I gave it to everyone as a gift. It was not only a spectacular view of us from the moon, but elegant evidence that revealed how we were all living together, without visible fences or borders, on one blue, wet, beautiful ball.)

NASA had planned a live broadcast from around the moon, anticipating the largest audience ever listening to a human voice. As I sat in my boyfriend's car on this Christmas Eve, helicopter lights glaring, music blaring, I listened, too. They chose to read from the book of Genesis. And just as one astronaut began, "In the beginning..." the helicopter lights switched off, the music stopped, the lights downtown dimmed, and it got very quiet. He continued:

"God created the heaven and the earth. And the earth was without form and void and darkness was upon the face of the deep. And the spirit of God moved upon the face of the waters. And God said, 'Let there be light.' And there was light. And God saw the light. And it was good."

MORE...

Reversing the direction you look can open up a whole new way of thinking, being, and feeling. It can also dislodge old ideas, unnecessary assumptions, and useless habits. A newborn baby sees the world upside down because it takes some time for the baby's brain to learn to turn the picture right side up. When we turn ourselves upside down we let go of preconceptions. It opens the way for the unexpected and allows us to change our viewpoints. When you are outside of your box you get to discover another side of yourself. And, it is good.

CHAPTER 4

Heartfelt

Gestures

51—SAVING GRACE

Place one hand on your belly, over your navel. Now place the other hand over your heart. Remember, your heart is almost in the center of your chest, slightly to the left side. With some gentle pressure, massage your heart area, using small circles with the palm of your hand. Encourage your hand to also stimulate the soft tissue under your collarbone. Now make small circles over your belly. Vigorously combine the movements and massage using both hands for one full minute.

 MORE...

Grace has many definitions. One meaning is compassion and kindhearted treatment, usually in the care of others. It is valuable to save some grace for ourselves, too. With hand on belly and heart treat yourself kindly by touching, connecting, and being conscious of two profound areas of your body and emotional being.

Your belly is a place of nourishment, where you take in and digest food and experience from outside of yourself. Many cultures see the belly as the home of the ego. It represents who we are in society and symbolizes our accomplishments, power, and productivity. When we have "gut" feelings we are often getting a strong intuition from in here about the world out there.

Your heart is a place of nourishment as well, but its nourishment is love, forgiveness, kindness, and compassion. Often, when we feel someone's joy or sorrow we find ourselves automatically bringing our hand to our heart and holding it there for a minute. That's where we sense heartache, feel our hearts warming, or racing, or pumping like mad.

Stimulating your belly and heart areas is also a way to feed your brain. Your brain, which is only one-fiftieth of your body weight, uses one-fifth of its oxygen. This massage encourages fresh oxygen to be pumped into your digestive tract, bloodstream, and brain. This simple activity has profound results.

52—FINGERS ON THE PULSE

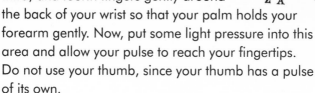

Place the fingers of your dominant hand on the opposite wrist. For a solid connection try wrapping the index, third, and fourth fingers gently around the back of your wrist so that your palm holds your forearm gently. Now, put some light pressure into this area and allow your pulse to reach your fingertips. Do not use your thumb, since your thumb has a pulse of its own.

Take a moment to make contact with your heartbeat. Close your eyes and allow yourself to spend a full two minutes sensing the rhythm, how your heart beats without the need to control it, the power and depth of the rhythm and energy, the aliveness of your very being. Breathe quietly so that you can hear the sounds coming from the inside out.

Heartache

I went to visit someone I was in love with. But things weren't working out very well. It was really confusing and sad. After a few days of emotional chaos, I came down with a 103-degree fever. I felt like I was going to die. I couldn't breathe. I couldn't swallow. I couldn't cry.

I went to the emergency room. They gave me a chest X-ray. The doctor called me in to examine the results. He pointed to a gray mass hovering over my left lung. "You have pneumonia," he told me. "You see this strange mass hanging heavy right over your heart? That's congestion. I've never seen it mirror the shape of a human heart so closely."

He called in a young resident who asked me a bunch of questions: Did I smoke? No. Did I take drugs? No. Had I been exposed to a sick person? No.

I told him it may not sound very scientific, but my heart had recently been broken, and although I was really sad, I just couldn't cry. I told him all my tears felt stuck, weighing heavy over my left lung. The resident looked quizzically at the X-ray. "You mean that dark shadow is actually an image of your heartache?" The older doctor shook his head in disbelief. "That's impossible. You can't take a picture of a broken heart."

The resident and I locked eyes. We both knew my sorry emotional state was hanging right there, fully illuminated for all to see, on the metal light stand.

 **MORE...**

Our hearts beat about one hundred thousand times in a single day. By heartbeats, a life is not brief. And rarely is a beat missed. But usually we aren't aware of any of this. Coming to your pulse means you are connecting to the present moment. You are here and now. There's no way to hide.

We all pledged allegiance to the flag and were told, "Put your hand on your heart." It seemed so intimate and slightly embarrassing at first as we placed our hand on our chest and felt the rhythm and beat of our life force.

Our own heartbeat reassures us we are well. We dread that one day it will stop. There are hundreds of phrases to describe our emotional state using the word heart. My heart is broken. How do you really feel, in your heart? Of course we know love and passion do not live in one organ, or any organ. Yet there is no need to explain. We can feel it when our hearts are light and full of love. Or heavy and filled with lead. We know when they are breaking, swelling, leaping, or sinking.

Although the heart was once considered the center of the body, in the last century Western science has given the throne over to the brain. But current research has discovered that the EKG, or electrocardiogram, the curve traced on a visual printout to diagnose heart health, sets the EEG, or electroencephalogram, the graphic record of the brain. So our heart rate sets the tone for our brain pulses. That means the heart is really the core, the central pacemaker, and if the heart is coherent the brain is coherent. Feel into your heart and recognize the miraculous access you have as you touch your core simply by placing fingers on wrist!

53—BEAT YOUR PULSE

Now reconnect with your pulse again, but this time pay closer attention to the exact rhythm or beating pattern. It helps to speak the beats aloud. Medical textbooks describe the sound of the heartbeat as "Lupp-dupp." Say, "Lupp-dupp, lupp-dupp." Find the beat. Now that you have the rhythm in your mind, make fists and reproduce the beats using your desk, the floor, a book, or even your chest as a drum.

After a little while, speed up the rhythm by pounding or drumming twice as fast. Then retake your pulse to reconnect with it and drum again, but this time slow it way down.

 MORE...

Drumming mirrors your heartbeat. You are a rhythm keeper. Your body has many internal rhythm sections including your heartbeat, breathing patterns, brain waves, the ebb and flow of your cerebral spinal fluid, and your digestion. Beating your heartbeat helps release your emotions and prepares you for deep relaxation. It also brings an almost immediate innate sense of safety, carrying you directly from head to heart, without a lot of thinking or doing.

54—BELLY BREATHER STRESS BUSTER

Sitting comfortably in a chair, put both feet on the floor and take a deep breath. Inhale as though your belly is an inflatable balloon. Fill it up and push it out. It might help to put your hand on your belly and feel it pulling away from your body. Hold for three full seconds. Exhale softly out of your mouth for five seconds. Watch your belly drop back down into your spine.

Inhale again, but this time concentrate on the cool sensation of the air as it rushes into your nostrils. Exhale audibly through your mouth, just as you might when blowing dust softly off a mirror, and empty your belly as you feel the warmth of the air against your lips. The belly breath is a great way to help you relax, let go of tension, and settle yourself into focus or rest.

(By the way, if you need more help learning how to fill up your belly, try lying down and placing a book on your stomach. You can watch your belly expand like a balloon more easily when there's something balanced on top of it.)

 MORE...

One breath is all that keeps us on this narrow path between living and dying. And each day the world passes over 23,000 breaths in and out of our bodies. If you are feeling off, out of sorts, or tired, there is a good chance you have less oxygen in your brain than you need. Breathing changes the mix in your system. It adds oxygen and cleans out the cobwebs. And it is always available to you.

Our breathing reflects every emotional or physical effort and every disturbance. When someone is breathing hard or fast (and has not just exercised), it is often a sign of anxiety, paranoia, or real fear. Breathing is the key for handling emergency situations. When you can control your respiration you can control your body's accelerator. That means you can control how you feel and respond to stress.

In neural linguistic programming there is a technique developed to create rapport with another person. What you do is listen to the pattern of another's breathing and mirror it in yourself. This allows the other person to unconsciously feel more at ease. Rapid breathing rattles our chain. One way to handle the discomfort of being around that kind of anxious energy is to breathe back slowly and evenly.

 SNAP TO YOUR IMAGINATION

55—BREATHE UNDERWATER

Pretend you are weightless, floating in a river, lake, or ocean. With no effort, buoyant, and in silence, pretend you are sinking gently underwater and can breathe easily. You take in a big breath of air through the water itself and soar through the depths. You are free.

56—HEAD TO EARTH

When sitting at your desk, lower your eyes and slowly roll your head down, bringing your forehead to rest gently on the desk. Make contact with the place your hairline begins. If you want to make this bow a more complete move, kneel on the carpet and bring your head down to touch the symbolic ground. Either way, you are making contact with Earth. Bob your head three times and then make contact. Linger with or without eyes closed, breathe, and notice how this makes you feel.

 MORE...

Bowing is an ancient and highly stylized gesture. Whether we cast ourselves down to the ground or make an abbreviated motion with our heads, the act of supplication humbles us to another, to Nature, to God. We've all seen people prostrate themselves in worship or pay reverence to someone important. Monks bow all of the time, to one another, to their teachers, and to statues that represent powerful deities.

Bowing is a way of making ourselves smaller. Not only do we shrink down in size, but as we lower our eyes and hide our faces we are also saying, "I am small before you," as we honor something or someone larger than ourselves.

This posture of submission is an opportunity to make direct contact with Earth. Connecting our forehead to the ground is deeply satisfying. It creates a sense of trust and awe, and has been proven to slow the heartbeat. It is beautiful to kneel and kiss the ground, acknowledging with our physical form all of the gifts that make up our rich lives.

There is also a special stage in the development of a baby in which you find him or her rolling on the head from a kneeling position. Often you'll discover babies sleeping so comfortably with their heads supported face down. Babies intuitively know how comforting it is to rest in this gathered-in position. The folded kneeling induces a feeling of intimacy with themselves. They naturally feel protected from the world, in a state of nonverbal serenity. The sensation of anchoring the head in the ground is a rare experience for an adult. Pressure against solid ground reminds us of the joy of rolling and resting as a child. And our tired necks will thank us as well.

57—INNER HAPPY FACE

Place your attention on your lips, mouth, and corners of your mouth. Relax your face and feel yourself in a neutral, nonexpressive state. Now, ever so slightly, raise the corners of the mouth until you feel the beginning of a tiny smile. Allow the corners of your mouth to remain in this uplifted position and turn your attention to your eyes. First, notice them as they are in their neutral, relaxed state. Then, ever so slightly, raise the corners of the eyes until you feel your eyes smiling too. The corners of the eyes and mouth should now feel like one unit. You may notice that placing your face in this small smile radiates a distinct, warm sense of wellbeing. This feeling is the inner happy face.

Play around with your smile until it is barely perceptible on the outside but still feels like a happy expression on the inside. Sense what that does to your mood. Now imagine you are smiling in your belly. Then bring a smile to your heart, lungs, and any other part of your body.

Say Cheese

Here he comes. It's my Uncle Harry and his black Brownie box camera. He's all wound up in wires and flashes and I'm supposed to stand like a statue. He has me pose by the new chartreuse chair or the peach tree, and he says "Hunny Bunny, smile like a movie star." I am usually cranky. So Uncle Harry begs me: "Come on, say 'cheese.'" I say, "Munster. Swiss. Jack," and scrunch up my nose like a sourpuss. He fidgets and begs me again: "What kind of face is that? Come on. Say 'money.'"

I refuse. "Please, just press the button already."

And then of course he says, "Say 'boys'" and I finally make the kind of smile he is waiting for, and happily, he snaps and flashes his camera and lights his big cigar. "You are some cutie, Hunny Bunny."

MORE...

Have you ever walked down the street worrying about your relationships, your job, your whole life? Then you glance up and notice someone is smiling at you. And in a split-second you find you are smiling back. You've suddenly dropped your troubles, stood up a little taller, and walked on knowing everything was going to be okay. A genuine smile has tremendous power.

The Taoists in ancient China taught that cultivating an inner smile, a smile to oneself, insured health, happiness, and longevity. Why? Smiling to yourself is like basking in love: you become your own best friend. Living with an inner smile is living in harmony with yourself. That's because you are happier when you are already smiling. Emotion follows physiological changes as much as physiological changes follow emotion. Although this view of emotions is counterintuitive, it makes sense. You can elevate your mood by smiling. It may seem like the tail wagging the dog, but so what? Wagging tails mean happy dogs! And if that doesn't convince you, smile just to give your body a break. It takes only seventeen muscles to make a smile, but a frown uses more than double that—a whopping forty-three!

58—ON THE TIP OF YOUR TONGUE

Lick your lips, swallow, stick out your tongue. Move around inside your mouth with your tongue. Now, let

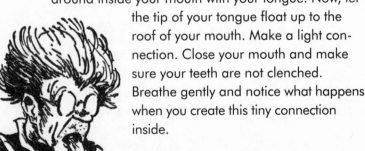

the tip of your tongue float up to the roof of your mouth. Make a light connection. Close your mouth and make sure your teeth are not clenched. Breathe gently and notice what happens when you create this tiny connection inside.

How to French Kiss

Susan, the smartest girl in the class, came over to work on our science project. Our assignment was to create something that would help the kids understand puberty. Susan and I collected a bunch of snails from the garden. We built a little house for them and fed them lettuce three times a day. One day, while feeding them dinner, Susan whipped out a movie magazine and pointed to the cover. Liz Taylor and Richard Burton were dressed in their elaborate costumes from *Cleopatra* and were intertwined and kissing. Susan told me they were French kissing.

"What is that?" I asked.

Susan explained. She used a black and red marker to illustrate. Liz's tongue, illustrated with a red dotted line, was in Richard's mouth; and Richard's tongue, illustrated with a black dotted line, was in Liz's mouth. I couldn't believe it! Why would they do a thing like that?

On Friday we took our display to class, lined up our snails, and one by one, poured salt on them. Nothing happened for a few minutes and everyone got restless. Then it happened. All of the snails foamed up, bubbled, and were gone. All that was left were empty shells.

"That's what puberty is," Susan announced. "One day you wake up and the old you has totally disappeared."

The teacher smiled, but quickly her attention was drawn away. There was a big commotion in the room. A boy named Larry had gotten hold of Susan's magazine, and he and a girl named Sara were busy pretending to be Richard and Liz. Puberty and snails were no longer the focus. The teacher sternly said, "This is science, not art class. Better figure out the difference!"

She confiscated the magazine, but not soon enough. I suspect a good half of the kids decided then and there that art was a far more exciting calling!

 MORE...

The tongue is one of our strongest muscles, but usually we don't use it unless talking or kissing. There are many pressure points and glands located in your palate. When stimulated by your tongue they give a subtle energy boost. As you release the tongue you feel a vibration at the back of your neck and a wave of relaxation.

In Tantric yoga the tongue is considered a kind of control mechanism or switch. Not only does its immobilization silence the chatter of the busy mind, but tongue to palate completes a circuit in the body's flow of life force that awakens the pineal gland in the inner brain. It produces a divine nectar which stimulates the body's production of endorphins, neurotransmitters that lead to a sense of inner calm and wellbeing. Check it out for yourself.

59—PRAYER HANDS

Sitting in a chair or standing, lift your chest, keeping your shoulders back and down. Lightly join the fingertips of both hands together in prayer fashion, as though a small ball floats inside your palms. Place your hands together in front of your chest, fingers pointing slightly away from you. Lightly press together the palms, especially focusing on the balls of your hands (where the lower knuckles meet the palm). Repeat the light pressure two or three times. Now close your eyes, allow your hands to float lightly, with delicate pressure, in front of your heart, and breathe. To complete, you may wish to bow your head slightly and touch your forehead to the tips of your fingers.

Soul Nose

My girlfriend Harriet's guinea pig Burry died. Annie, the housekeeper, conducted a formal burial service. First she stuffed wads of cheesecloth into her nostrils and then ours. Annie told us when you bury someone, you need to protect your soul from mingling with the soul of the deceased. Souls escape through noses. Then Annie sneezed. A chill ran up my spine. Annie wasn't phased. She was too busy inside this fancy ritual.

She got down on her knees and collected dust from under all of the rugs and behind the refrigerator. She told us the dust you find around your house is really a mixture of creatures that once walked the earth, so cleaning is a very spiritual experience. She put the little pig into a shoebox and sprinkled some of the dust all over his furry little body. She put her hands into prayer pose and instructed us to do the same. Harriet and I touched our fingertips to our foreheads as we joined Annie in singing "Ashes to ashes. Dust to dust."

Annie buried the pig out in the backyard next to the peach tree. She snapped the cheesecloth out of her nose and told us to spit on the grave. "Spittle contains a little bit of the best part of your soul. Now let's bow our heads in silence, hands together, girls, over your heart, and let's all spit again." Harriet, Annie, and I spit in unison. "Now Burry will get a really good send-off."

MORE...

Prayer is a harmonious expression that includes body, mind, and soul. By concentrating with reverence and focus, you take the outgoing energies of your being and pull them inside. In a sense, you transform from the world of matter into the world of spirit. Even if you haven't prayed in years, or ever, this universal prayer pose seems to be a natural way of bringing yourself into a place of silence and reverie. It also helps you open your chest and heart to the world. When the palms are pressed together it is symbolic of unity and oneness with all people and with our notion of God. In Chinese medicine this pose is said to balance and neutralize our yin—the darker internal side—and our yang—the brighter external side.

Through prayer you connect to the Absolute, God, Allah, the universal part of ourselves, the life force, the Goddess, Gaia, Nature. It does not matter to whom you pray. It is more important that you have a willingness to simply participate in the mystery of being.

Heartfelt gestures celebrate and honor our aliveness. They refer to heart in the biggest sense of the word. With an infinite openness to whatever is, we smile at the deep mystery of being and take joy in the next breath.

60—Sacred Password

Extend your arms to the sides with soft elbows, your palms up. You are opening your arms to the sky. You can do this sitting or standing. Be aware of the space above you. Gaze upward gently, in a posture of praise and adulation. This is a very physical way of letting yourself feel that there is a Greater Power. Breathe softly and recite aloud a favorite prayer, poem, or word that brings comfort and peace. When you are finished you may want to bring your hands together in prayer fashion to rest.

Password

I went to the hospital to visit my grandfather, Papa, who'd had a heart attack. I stood at the foot of his bed while the TV flickered behind me. It hung from the ceiling, so Papa could look at it and me at the same time. I could see the game show *Password* reflected across his bifocals. Alan Ludden, the host, was saying, "Something you wear..." and Papa told me he was tired and had had enough of life. A few contestants on TV got really excited. I think they had won the round.

My grandfather reached for my hand. "Don't forget our password," he winked. I whispered a Hebrew prayer into his ear, one that he taught me long ago. He smiled. "Yes, that's the one."

I loved him. I remembered how when Kennedy died my grandfather decided to quit smoking. The day of the funeral he stood by our big TV and crushed the life out of his last cigar. Now in the hospital I turned off the TV so that I could look into his eyes. They glistened more brightly now that the game show wasn't flickering across his glasses.

His eyes glowed with a magical light that he carried inside of him. I repeated our password: "Sh'ma Israel, Adonai Elohainu, Adonai Ehad,"and then my Papa went to sleep.

 MORE...

When addressing a deity or something sacred, some people automatically stretch their arms out wide to the sky, inviting the divine presence in, as if through some kind of funnel. This is not very discreet, but feels very welcoming. Combining this physical invitation to the divine with a sacred password creates a potent vehicle of body and voice that takes you into a magical inner world.

We use words all day long, so we tend to forget their impact and beauty. But the sounds of people's names, the names of God, and special syllables and word combinations have the power to transport us to altered states that help us appreciate the sacred in our lives. Chanting, humming, toning, and speaking meaningful or symbolic words out loud has great value and power. They are all ways of praying, ways of using words and sounds to take us to another level.

Choose a sound or word that you love and can live with. Consider what is beautiful about the classic words of power and creativity: OM, Alleluia, Allah, Elohim, Aloha. What is so profound about these sounds? Now say your word over and over again. How does it make you feel? Notice how the word creates vibrations in your head and activates the hard palate of the mouth, making it resonate. You can ask people you like what is the most beautiful sound they have ever heard. What word reminds you of truth? Use their insights as your sacred password. And sometimes after repeating these words we can truly hear, truly listen to, truly experience the still, small voice of that which is most sacred.

61—FOREHEAD STRETCH

Cross your forearms over one another in front of your face. Now with each index finger gently and slowly outline your eyebrows (left finger on right eyebrow, right finger on left eyebrow). Now wiggle your fingers a little bit above the center of each brow, midway to your hairline. You will notice a slight indentation on your forehead. Lightly rest three fingers of each hand on this spot. With focus, pull the forehead up in a slightly taut position, and close your eyes. Take five to ten slow, deep breaths.

 *MORE...*

The forehead is an area that covers the frontal lobes, the more rational, thinking portion of our brains. When we are overwhelmed or stuck we often slide into a fight or flight mode and lose touch with our reasoning capacities. By stretching the forehead up and relaxing our face, we diffuse the primitive reflex to bolt or lash out and, in so doing, release emotional stress. Touching these points moves the brain response from the middle or emotional part of the brain to the front, allowing a more rational thought process. It also relaxes the muscles of expression under the forehead skin that often freeze into a state of anger, anxiety, worry, or concern.

62—CURTSEY LIKE A BALLERINA

Curtsey Like a Ballerina.
Make Your Curtain Call.

CHAPTER 5

Daily Grind

63—OPPOSITES

Do something different. Leave the house five minutes early, and linger somewhere pretty on your way to the office. Eat ice cream for breakfast. Wear purple socks. Work only at night. Have sex in the middle of the day. Don't wear a wristwatch. Sleep on the other side of the bed. If you always read the newspaper, don't.

T-Bone Wisdom

I was eating lunch in a coffee shop. I ordered a grilled chicken salad and leaned against the wall of the padded booth. I wore an olive green baseball cap, black sweatshirt, black jeans, and sunglasses, even though it was dark inside.

A very old couple sat down behind me. Each of them appeared at least 100 years old, and although bent over and very wrinkled, both wore contemporary clothes and seemed quite alive. They ordered steak, he decaf, she regular coffee, and two slices of custard pie. He began to flip through a dessert menu and read the names of all the pies out loud. She scanned the throw-away section of the newspaper that was plastered with ads for appliance sales. He had reached P for peach and pecan when she interrupted: "You know, you've got to stop with saying, 'I'm asleep. I'm asleep,' all the time. It's not good for you and you know it. Start saying 'I'm awake, I'm awake,' instead."

The old guy sighed and said, "I try, but I always end up saying I'm asleep." Then he began again with S for strawberry. I moved slightly and startled her.

"I didn't know you were there," she smiled at me.

"I'm hiding," I answered.

"Someone as pretty as you shouldn't be hiding," she said as the T-bones arrived. "Show up." She turned back to her husband and shook him a little. He picked up a fork. "Try eating with the other hand. Come on. Put the fork in your left hand. That will keep you awake!"

The old guy put the fork in his left hand, struggled a moment, and swooped some mashed potatoes into his mouth. He let out a loud laugh!

It was definitely one of those moments when I knew I needed to be all ears. "Stay awake. Stay awake. Don't hide. Show up." This tiny ancient woman with bright blue eyes and a little velvet cap was sawing her steak in the middle of nowhere and spouting truths.

 *MORE...*

Don't wait until you are 100 years old to start waking up. Start using the other side of your body, start using the other side of your brain, your heart, even your soul. Intentionally vary some habits. You can begin with something simple such as using your nondominant hand more often. If you always brush your teeth with one hand, use the other. If that isn't interesting enough, try parting your hair on the opposite side of your head. And the next time someone asks you, "How are you?" don't answer, "Fine."

Much of the joy of traveling is seeing different sights, smelling different air, hearing other voices and other languages. But you can experience all that right where you live. Just start changing some habits. Put your TV in the closet for a month, and have an interesting conversation with someone in person. Break out of the prison of familiarity by disrupting your habitual patterns. And welcome the discomfort. It's a sign you are snapping out of it!

64—Slow Motion

Wash your hands in slow motion. Instead of grabbing the soap and rub-a-dub-dubbing, track every single

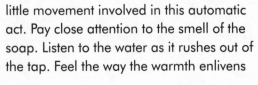 little movement involved in this automatic act. Pay close attention to the smell of the soap. Listen to the water as it rushes out of the tap. Feel the way the warmth enlivens

your fingers. Notice the soap bubbles forming and glistening under the lights. There are endless pieces to this seemingly mundane puzzle. Examine and stretch out the moment. Soak in the pleasure of this sensual delight and maybe it will make the next three thousand times you hit the sink a bit more enjoyable.

 SNAP TO YOUR IMAGINATION

65—FLOATING ON AIR

Pretend you are a cloud. You dance across the sky, change shape and form. You smell ten thousand scents as they make their way through the air, absorbing your favorites. You can come and go as you please. You are unpredictable. You are lightness.

66—FOLLOW YOUR NOSE

Put something on your desk or in your hands that really smells good. What gets you going? Cinnamon, a sprig of basil, freshly roasted coffee beans, or a sweet red rose? It's probably not onions or hard-boiled eggs, but it could be a cheeseburger and fries. Or a sweater that belongs to someone you adore. Keep a selection of favorite smells stored in plastic bags nearby and open them up now and then for a wonderful whiff, or a trip down memory lane.

No More Basil, Garlic, or Gasoline

My friend's nose stopped working. He told me it was a subtle loss. Not like losing your hearing or eyesight. It was insidious, slow to surface or identify. But one day he realized his life was flat. Varied, distinct, good, bad, or memorable smells no longer punctuated his life.

The whole mess started when he began teaching painting and drawing at a new high school. Like most art rooms, it was the lost attic—fifty years' collection of someone else's treasures. The storage room was stacked floor to ceiling with old junk, and everything was covered with dust and rat droppings. He began the daunting but necessary task of making sense of the space, trying to find room for the things he needed, and tossing out the things he didn't.

As he reached the uppermost shelves, an avalanche of dust and old vermin droppings covered his head, sending him into an immediate asthmatic seizure. It developed into a miserable three-week sinus infection. After a ton of antibiotics, the infection seemed to be clearing. To celebrate he took a bike ride and was overcome by a series of scents jumping out to reach him—cedar chips, barbecue smoke, lawn trimmings, night-blooming jasmine, and the earthy aroma of wet dirt. He told me he was smiling from the onslaught of life's aroma.

But the next few days he noticed something odd. Every morning as he'd grind his morning coffee, he'd find himself strangely disconnected from the task at hand. He'd sip his coffee and it tasted like bad water. When he'd slather on some rich-smelling pear hand lotion, he felt somehow cut off again. The lotion lost its signature. His olfactory nerves were shot and no matter how hard he licked or sniffed, it was over. He confessed he felt a profound sense of entropy. He began to empathize with a three-legged, blind-in-one-eye junkyard dog, probably named "Lucky," who went deaf overnight. Except, of course, Lucky could still smell.

Grieving his loss, he made a list of smells he missed the most. He painted them in large green letters on his bedroom wall. They included: spoiled milk, an unlit pilot light, his wife's hair, night blooming jasmine, the solvent from the old mimeograph machines, oaken Chardonnay, sweaty smelly socks, garlic and basil and olive oil, gasoline at the pump, mildewed wetsuits, sunscreen, and the ocean.

He went filled with hope to a specialist. People get back their sight and hearing, why not their sense of smell? But the German nose specialist looked downcast as he gazed into my friend's eyes and told him: "Vonce ze smell goez, it rarely comes back."

MORE...

Smells go straight to the brain. The human nose can identify over ten thousand smells, and any one of them can trigger grief, nostalgia, or joy in a nanosecond. That's because the smell and memory center in the brain are neighbors. We are carried across time and space in an instant. Many passionate and memorable relationships begin with a sniff of perfume on a shoulder. The same scent smelled days or years later can transport us out of the moment and into deep ineffable reverie.

When we smell, we are touching the world in an immediate way. Scent is elemental and pungent, overflowing with impact and memory. Remember your first scents? Maybe your grandmother's apple pie crisping up in the oven, linseed oil with paint swirling on a canvas, a lilac in spring?

Western culture tends to give primacy to vision, and then hearing. But the other senses don't go directly to the brain in the way that smell does. They wander around through a number of switchboards and networks, distilled and interpreted before triggering a response. But smell has a direct line. It hits home immediately and then transports us down memory lane.

Smell and taste make life a heady and succulent feast. Without them we would be impoverished. Smell and taste instantly call up heart-stopping memories. They fill us with the rich scent of coffee and the mouth-watering flavor of chocolate. Smell and taste also link us to loved ones. Licking a lover's neck or sniffing our mother's perfume feeds deep primal connections that never disappear.

67—It Dissolves

Watch something dissolve. Try some sugar in your hot tea. How about milk in your coffee? Just watch. Where does it all go? Notice how it tends to swirl in a circle. And then it's gone. As you watch let the stress and tension in your body, your jaw, your eyes, your mind dissolve as well. Take a deep breath and just disappear.

QUICK SNAP

68—BUTTON AND UNBUTTON

Button and Unbutton Your Shirt Three Times in a Row

69—MOUTH WATERING

Put a piece of candy into your mouth. Feel the texture of jellybean, lemon drop, peanut-butter cup. Let it linger. Feel how it starts to melt when it touches the warmth of your tongue. Roll it over and under your tongue. Feel the juices or creamy chocolate melt around your cheeks and soak it in without swallowing for a tiny second longer than usual. Savor it. Be aware of how the sweetness makes you feel. The brain thrives on glucose. This is pure sugar, a form of soul nutrition. Delight in the depths of what is often a forgotten experience.

Certs

I was riding on a bus filled with classmates on a teen-tour across America. Steven, a quiet boy with big green eyes and neatly parted black hair, sat next to me. As the bus swerved out of the parking lot in Chicago, headed to Philadelphia, Steven leaned over to kiss me. I got dizzy and warm watching his mouth coming toward me. Before he made contact, he popped a little round white Certs into his mouth. The aroma of the pepper-mint made my head spin. And then he kissed me.

"Ick," I thought. It wasn't the kiss that grossed me out; it was the Certs. Somehow, the fact that Steven needed to suck on a mint before kissing me made me queasy. At twelve, I already knew that this handsome boy was convinced he wasn't good enough. He felt compelled to cover himself up with what I thought of as the aroma of old ladies and bad Christmas celebrations. The aroma conjured up in me a seemingly endless supply of bad peppermint memories.

I bolted out of my seat, nearly sending Steven's head into the window. I retreated to the back of the bus, where I found Barbara sprawled out on the long back seat. She had giant breasts, wore white lipstick, and was dressed suggestively. I told her Steven had kissed me.

"Did you kiss him back?" she smiled.

"Of course not!" I shrieked.

"You should have," she scolded. "You'll never run out of kisses."

She was right. I paused. "But Barbara," I whined, "he popped a Certs in his mouth a second before he kissed me. Ick!"

Barbara shook her head in disgust. "Double ick," she agreed. "But next time ask him for one too. That way, at least you'll be on the same wavelength."

MORE...

We live in a wash of smells and tastes. Molecules float back into the nasal cavity behind the bridge of the nose. They are absorbed by mucosa containing receptor cells bearing tiny hairs called cilia. Five million of these take the fragrance right in. The olfactory bulb gets it, signals the cerebral cortex, and sends a message straight to the limbic system. That's the ancient center of emotion and creativity that houses inklings for lust, longing, and the entire palette of human feelings.

When we smell and taste, there is very little interpretation necessary. Bingo, there is an immediate response. Smell in particular leaps over the language center of the brain into pure visceral experience. With less time to reflect or edit, it instantly triggers a string of emotions, images, and memories.

In spite of its potent effect on us, most of us rarely take the time to smell or taste our food. Watch people in restaurants. How many actually dare to lean down to inhale the scent of their pasta or lamb chop? Is it just too much for us to digest? Would life be too rich if we really got engaged? Find out. Next time you order a yummy plate of pasta with garlic, onions, and tomatoes take a deep, slow sniff, close your eyes, and immerse yourself in the depths of the delicious aromas. It does not take anything away from your visual or auditory awareness to pay attention to smell or taste. In fact, all the senses enrich the others if you just let them.

70—WATCH WATER BOIL

CHAPTER 6

Make Your Mark!

71—STROKE YOUR PET

Gaze at your hands in great detail, finger by finger. Look at your nails, the fronts and the backs. Consider how many hands you have shaken or held. Remember five people, animals, or things you've caressed, stroked, or treasured that make you smile. Don't forget the worry beads, polished stones, or sports putty.

Now imagine you are stroking a pet. It can be a memory of a pet long gone, a current pet, or a pet you wish you had. It can be a kitten, a boa, a mouse, even a fish. Or find your current pet and make a special effort to have a daily stroking session.

 MORE...

Petting or stroking is a natural, healing gesture. It transmits a feeling of pure, direct love. Just stroking someone's hand or neck lowers the blood pressure of both lucky parties. Touch is nourishment. It doesn't matter if you are petting feathers, scales, spines, or claws—make contact. It has been proven that people with pets are calmer and happier, and live longer.

Petting releases bonding hormones called oxytocin and prolactin, which create higher levels of serotonin, the neurotransmitter which protects against depression. And depression is often considered a way of losing touch, with yourself, with what you love, with your expression. Keep on stroking!

72—Magnetic Hands

Hold your hands in front of your belly, about a foot apart. Let your palms face each other. Now take a few minutes and notice the sensations in your hands as you slowly move them closer together, then farther apart. Play around with changing the space between your palms. Don't let your hands touch! Simply be curious about what there is to sense.

As you experience this sensation, think of any words that might describe it. Strong. Soft. Fluffy. Warm. Magnetic. Tickling. Soothing.

Mustang Magnetism

It was early evening. He drove me to the park in his convertible Mustang, turned off the ignition, spun around in his seat and exclaimed, "Have you done the hand thing?" I got nervous.

"What hand thing?" I tried to smile to cover up my obvious lack of imagination and experience.

"Here." He reached out his left hand, flexed back at the wrist, and took my right hand, bending it back to match his. Our palms faced one another about a foot apart, his larger fingers lined up evenly with my little stubbies. I noticed how nicely his nails were cut. Instinctively, I felt an urge to place my hand on his, but he pulled back. "This isn't about the obvious!"

I felt confused, but then he gently eased his palm closer to mine, ever so slowly, until they hovered near one another, about two inches apart. "Now, come a little closer," he whispered. "But really feel what's happening. Move real, real slowly...and don't touch."

I liked this boy. He was different. And I really liked how this thing felt. There were so many sensations. A warm heat and an electronic pulsing. A mysterious humming vibration and a thick magnetic pull. Our breath fogged the windows as I sat there silently in a trance, gazing out at the lights from the city. It was like all of the energies of nature converged and were articulated in this tiny but profound gesture.

"What you feel is the life force!" He spoke with authority and tossed his head back. "This is so cool." He laughed. This boy loved being alive. I jumped up and kissed him, right on the lips. Enough science and big ideas for one night!

 **MORE...**

What is this energy? Or is it a substance? Martial arts experts and Chinese medicine call it Chi, the life force. It is used to sense danger, what an attacker's next move will be. It can also be used for healing in therapies such as Chi Gong and acupuncture. Most people have the sensitivity to feel this magnetism if they give themselves a chance. But they rarely explore, so they don't perceive.

You may feel tingling or a sensation that the space between your hands is like taffy, a kind of elastic. It may seem like there is a ball of energy between your hands, or arcs of subtle electricity flowing. When your hands are within several inches of each other, one of the sensations you feel is heat, physical heat. It is something we often sense but do not identify in daily life.

Physiological research has identified infrared sensors in the skin, which tell you when something hot is nearby. You can feel the warmth of the sun, or of a stove, and since human beings are almost 100 degrees (well, 98.6), you can also feel the heat of your own or another person's body from several inches away. Your body gives off heat that others can sense. Explore on your own and see what your range is for infrared.

73—FULL APPLAUSE

Applaud hard for a full two minutes. Now, shake your hands out,
as though you are brushing cobwebs away fast and furiously.

 MORE...

Applause is a fast and effective way to uplift your
spirits and stimulate your circulation. When you are
enthusiastic and want to give approval you just seem
to find yourself putting your hands together.

Applause is also contagious. When you applaud
good and long you often find yourself standing up,
and if you look around, so is everybody else. It's
called an ovation, but in a way, it's a physical rousing
that leads to cheering, hooting, and hollering.

Touch is as essential to human life as sunlight. And our hands are the masters of touch. They have such sensitivity. They open us up to the world on infinite levels.

It is said that the hand is the heart's landscape. With its twenty-six intricate bones, it is precise and agile, filled with the ability to do everything from the mundane to the sublime. Hands type, fold, dig, caress, pull, massage, express, tickle. They dial a phone, console a loved one, tie our shoes, make dinner, and give us a thrill. When we're lucky, we hold someone else's hand and create a nonverbal bridge of sensation and communication.

Making our mark links us to our deep history. As we scribble, draw, journal, we combine the senses and connect hand to heart. We touch the page and we hear our words and we see the newly discovered ideas unreel as we make the unknown known. Throughout time, hands have been considered the direct link to our souls. Palm readers are convinced our past and future are etched in our hands.

One of the very first subjects to be painted over thirty thousand years ago in limestone caves in Western Europe was the human hand. In these early cave paintings, no human form has yet been discovered, only hundreds of vivid positive and negative hand silhouettes. They are stenciled out- lines, in color, of actual Cro-Magnon hands, held against the wall.

74—DRAW GOD

Pick up a pencil, some crayons, or whatever is handy and draw God. That's right. Draw God. It sounds ridiculous. It sounds immoral. It sounds impossible. Just see what happens when you sit with a blank piece of paper and put something on it that represents God. Spend a good five minutes. Have some fun. If nothing else, draw a wonderful, big question mark.

If this is too much of a taboo, consider drawing something you see where you are. Just stare at the object, put your pencil or crayon on a piece of paper, and draw the image in one continuous line, without looking at your paper.

CBS Eye

The first image I remember seeing on TV was a black-and-white eyeball floating in a gray-and-white cross-hatched sky. It hovered inside the TV box for a long time while some guy did something called station identification. "This is KCBS, Los Angeles." I had no idea what station identification was.

When I went to Jewish nursery school at the local synagogue, our first assignment was to draw God. I drew what I later found out was the CBS logo.

 **MORE...**

In Zen training, koans are sometimes given to students to stretch their minds. A koan is an impossible question, such as "What is the sound of one hand clapping?" or "How can you stop the sun from rising?" or "What did your face look like before you were born?" There is no answer to the question, but wondering about it can break the hypnosis that words have over us. And, when we attempt something impossible and then give up, it creates room in our minds for new ways of thinking.

In the case of God, we have both a word and a concept. We think we know what this word refers to. Why, then, can you not make an image or a symbol that represents this concept just as the word God represents it? Ask yourself what issues this activity brings up. Where is your resistance? Is it in your head, hands, or heart?

75—YOUR NAME

Write your name over and over again. Fill a page. Write it fast. Write it slow. Now write all of your numbers down. Include your phone numbers, e-mail address, home address, social security number—you name it.

Left-Handed Smear

Being left-handed can be a mess. If you use a soft pencil
or a slightly wet pen, you not only smear the page as
you write but your entire left palm and your arm from
the pinkie to the elbow are covered with the remnants
of lead or ink. It was a real problem until I decided if I
couldn't beat it, I'd join it. So instead of being covered
in abstract streaks of color and smudges, I took great
delight in drawing elaborate patterns and shapes on my
right arm and hand. I could control those designs, so at
least one side of me would look artful!

I never realized the potential impact of this innocent
act. One Friday, I went to modern dance class and sat in
my usual place, front and center, facing the large floor-
to-ceiling mirrors. I sat in tailor fashion, with my arms
in a soft circle, ready to begin the floor work routine. In
marched my teacher, Fanya, a tiny, fiery Russian
woman. She walked in front of our line, nodding a
quick glance at each of us. When she got to me, she
turned white. She nearly fainted and had to grab the
barre against the wall to keep from falling.

"What is that?" she shouted as she stared at the fancy
ink work on my arm.

"It's just a design," I answered.

The teacher was boiling. "I thought it was a Jewish star tattooed on your arm. I saw it along with a number. It was as real as anything."

I was horrified that my self-conscious decision to cover up my embarrassment at being left-handed backfired and ended up hurting someone else.

MORE...

Our handwriting is truly unique, and our signatures even more so. But we tend to forget the power in a name and a number. And we often forget how amazing it is that we can make a bunch of wiggles on paper so that other people can read our deepest thoughts.

It's important to remember the magic of learning new words. And it's important to re-meet the words and numbers we use over and over again. When we look back on our lives and retrieve an old phone number, it's not just an empty series of numerals. It's a link to a piece of the past that has meaning and may even open up emotions and memories that might otherwise have been lost forever.

QUICK SNAP

76—CLENCH YOUR FIST

Clench Your Fist. Raise It High. Right On!

77—THE RIGHT HAND KNOWS WHAT THE LEFT HAND IS DOING

Draw the infinity sign over and over again. Don't hold the pencil too tightly. Large images are just fine. Do it with your dominant hand ten times. Do it with your opposite hand ten times. If possible, keep the move going up and around, rather than down and around. Now hold one pencil in each hand, put pencils on paper, and draw two infinity signs simultaneously, allowing one hand to lead while the other follows.

 *MORE...*

Hand-eye coordination defines how we do so many things. This bilateral drawing activity reorients you in space, brings your visual field together, and balances out both sides of the body. It also assists in opening up your chest and helps your arms and eyes. You will discover a rhythm and flow as you continue the move that will bring you into a sensation of connection and joy. It's just fun to use your body as you create an image.

78—Two Thumbs Up

Extend the thumbs straight out from the hands and curl the fingertips into the palms. Maintain a gentle pressure of tips on palms. Rest your hands on your thighs or your desk and feel the energy moving down your arms and out the tips of your thumbs. Now extend both arms out to the side with thumbs pointing up and try to relax. Do not bend your elbows. Maintain for one full minute, observing the impact on your breath, body, and mind.

MORE...

In our culture, two thumbs up is a sign of deep approval. It means "yes!" Italian paintings before the Renaissance used another common hand pose that was a more religious way of saying "yes." Hundreds of paintings feature a man usually touching his thumb to his index finger. This was called "kissing God." In the popular Neapolitan culture, the thumb symbolized God and the index finger symbolized the individual. In metaphysical India, the hand is a miniature universe representing a complete cosmological system. The thumb is often equated with the universal self and the rest of the fingers the individual, the ego, illusion, and worldly actions. When the entire hand is used in a gesture, it is said that all of creation is acted out, in an open, conscious, and loving fashion.

No matter the meaning, the very process of quietly holding a position that focuses on the hands creates focus and wellbeing. And the thumbs-up pose strengthens the nervous system while it calms the mind.

79—OPEN HEART, OPEN MIND

Press the tip of each thumb into the hollow space inside the middle of each armpit (right thumb to right armpit, left thumb to left armpit). Bring the palms parallel to the ground so the tips of the middle fingers of each hand just touch

together in front of your chest. The palms and fingers remain flat, open, straight, and parallel to the ground. Exert a slight pressure into the armpits, and allow the edges of the forefingers and thumbs to maintain slight pressure into the upper ribs and breast bone, almost mirroring the curved shape of the ribcage. Don't allow the hands to droop or the elbows to drop. Relax and maintain. Breathe easily.

 **MORE...**

Elaborate hand gestures carry different meanings in most cultures, including the ancient Chinese, Egyptian, Roman, Greek, Aborigine, Fijian, Inuit, Mayan, and Native American. In ancient India, hundreds of special hand gestures, called mudras, were created to guide energy flow and reflexes to the brain. By curling, crossing, stretching, and touching the fingers and hands, it was believed one could make a significant connection between the body and the mind.

Open Heart, Open Mind is a way to stand quietly at attention. It gives you an instant sense of power and focus as it opens up the chest, stabilizes the rib cage, and stimulates the circulation of oxygen into the heart and brain. Holding the pose, you might be amazed at how energized you feel as your entire body and mind wake up!

SNAP TO YOUR IMAGINATION

80—YOU ARE A CONDUCTOR

Pretend you are conducting a huge symphony orchestra. You are a dramatic and passionate conductor. You gesture grandly, with zest and vibrant energy, as you swoop your metal baton in the air to rhythms that stimulate and inspire. You command attention. You are powerful.

81—HAND WEB

Our hands do so much. They deserve a little time-out. A great way to release tension in your hands is to pinch the thick area of skin located at the web between your thumb and index finger. Take the forefinger and thumb of the opposite hand, find this tender spot, and apply firm pressure. Hold it a while and repeat with the other hand.

Boy's Hands

It was time to choose partners for the May Day dance. Although most kids automatically paired up, a batch of us just lurked in the background, trying to disappear. The teacher began to couple us up based on size. I was the shortest girl in the class so naturally I got stuck with the shortest boy. But there were two short boys, so I was stuck in between York and Guy.

We needed to skip in a circle for a while, then we had to bow to one another and rush in to grab a ribbon that hung from the maypole. York took my left hand and Guy my right and the skipping began. I had never held hands with a boy other than my little brother. I skipped fast and kept my gaze straight ahead as I tried to process the physicality of the experience. And I didn't like it.

York's little freckled hand was slippery wet. It was like trying to grasp a handful of wet egg noodles. But Guy's felt even worse. His hand had all kinds of crusty blisters running across the inside. I think he did a lot of chin-ups, but the fact that the blisters were hard-earned didn't make the experience of holding his hand any better. I couldn't believe it. The worse it felt the tighter they grabbed. Boy's hands. I just hoped whatever they had wasn't contagious.

82—PICK A WORD

Consider a favorite word. One that makes you feel good. Like "exquisite." Or something important like "forgiveness." Or maybe choose someone's name: "Beatrice." Or a quality of being: "grace." Or even a funny word that makes you laugh: "goiter."

Using your dominant hand, write this word in the air on a fake blackboard floating in front of you. Pretend your index finger is a piece of chalk and focus on the invisible word as you write it over and over again. Now, try switching hands and write it with your less dominant hand.

Mark My Word

There was some serious chatter reverberating on the playground. From the jungle gym to the tetherball court, kids were spreading the word. Now, this was no four-letter slang, it wasn't religious, and it certainly wasn't about who was with whom and who wasn't. It was antidisestablishmentarianism, the longest word any fourth grader had ever heard.

We loved saying it and we loved acting smart by throwing it into a casual sentence to impress our parents and teachers. We knew something they didn't. Well, sort of. No one really knew what it meant until little Vivian

Larner found it on page fifty-nine in the gigantic Oxford English Dictionary. The definition read: "A long word; Properly, opposition to the disestablishment of the Church of England." Huh? No matter, it was the first time most of us got a hint of how knowledge could be power and how power could make you feel...good.

Two years before, when I was in second grade, the teacher read out loud from a Dr. Seuss book called *On Beyond Zebra*. It was a story about an alphabet that existed long after the letter Z. I thought Z was as far as the alphabet could go.

I discovered all kinds of new letters like Beyondabit and WumbaGlikk. The hair on my neck stood up— "chicken skin," the teacher pointed out, as she finished the last sentence. Life beyond Zebra? There was suddenly much more to my day than boring old reality: "So on beyond Z! It's high time you were shown that you really don't know all there is to be known." The power of the word loomed large and life was never the same.

MORE...

Language is considered to be the greatest human invention. We have names for thousands upon thousands of physical objects in our lives. We also have names for the interactions between things and names for feelings that we experience within ourselves.

According to the Jewish liturgy the Bible says, "God spoke and the world came into being." Language is an act of creation. Whether it is musical language or mathematics, whenever you learn new words and ways of expressing yourself, you instantly open up to new ways of living, loving, and being.

CHAPTER 7

Jump on Your Bed

For these activities you'll need some common stuff you'll find around your house: A bed, flashlight, ball, magnifying glass, candle, rock, ice cube, and mirror.

83—Jump on Your Bed

Run into a bedroom—yours or someone else's—and jump on the bed. That's right. Climb up and have your way with the mattress and blankets and sheets. Make a little mess. Touch the ceiling if you can. You haven't forgotten how. It's just like riding a bike.

Raven Raucous

One day as I was about to enter a grocery store two ebony ravens were cawing above me high in the sky. They were playing an aerial acrobatic game. While the birds flew side-by-side, one called out three times as if to say, "Well, Buddy, watch this." Then he tucked in his wings, rolled over in 360-degree spirals, and fell about 200 feet straight toward the ground, righting himself just inches before his head hit the pavement. He peered right at me, radiating this totally recognizable expression of bird happiness, and he cawed really loud as if to say, "Hey, did you see that?" He repeated the acrobatics and got even fancier, sometimes rolling over four or more times before he'd right himself. When finished with his ten-point dive, he made another call and his partner, seemingly on cue, commenced to put on his own show. This must have lasted at least twenty minutes.

At some point my neck began to hurt, and I decided to go into the market. As I walked toward the door I noticed a trio of marauding blue jays committing a robbery in the parking lot. They had spotted a car with the groceries exposed from the open hatchback. One jay had already lifted up a bag of chips and was gleefully tearing them out of the bag. The other two were alternating keeping guard and plucking open a cooler.

Then the first jay was joined by three others, who together proceeded to pull an inflatable mattress nearly out of one of the car windows. As soon as the mattress poked out, they got real close together and started jumping on it like some kind of trampoline. They hopped from foot to foot, knocked each other's beaks, and bounced back and forth making these loud sounds that must have been bird belly-laughter.

I tossed some oatmeal cookie crumbs nearby, thinking I might distract them. But all of them became very still, didn't touch the crumbs, and stared at me for a long moment. Then they gurgled in disgust and got back to their gymnastics. I started to feel guilty. I think I'd have done better handing these guys a nice cool six-pack. That's probably what they were really after.

MORE...

Ravens belong to the family of birds called corvids. Corvids include blue jays and crows, those soulful and boisterous birds most of us think of as comics or pranksters. They represent a limited number of lucky creatures whose genes not only include the basics— such as eating, sleeping, mating, and nest building— but also have plenty of DNA dedicated to pure play.

Corvids devote huge chunks of their time to fun and frolic. All this goofing around has contributed to their enhanced brainpower, ingenuity, and large repertoire of flying patterns and sounds. Play breeds intelligence. It's a good idea to take their lead. Jump on your bed and play it for all it's worth. You won't get in trouble and you just might get smarter.

84—Light Show

Take out a flashlight and instead of using it to search for burglars in the night, take it to bed and have some fun. There's nothing as easy as creating a shadow show, since you really don't need anything but a flashlight and the dark. Get in bed and spin the light in circles on the ceiling. Look at yourself under the covers. Light up your index finger until it glows a surreal red. Make a shadow puppet—highlight something in the room so that it suddenly turns from very small to monster-size.

Shadow Play

I used to hang out at my girlfriend's house. We'd watch TV, snack on Jamoca Almond Fudge ice cream, and laugh ourselves into a tizzy. My friend's mom was Rita Hayworth. In those days, Rita was dating Prince Ali Khan. They had been married and divorced once already, but they were trying it again. It was remarkable watching this gin-and-tonic-filled lady in a blue frumpy housecoat transform herself into a glamorous movie star in no time flat. One night, she was watching TV with us and getting ready for her date at the same time. During every commercial break, she rushed upstairs and did something fancy with her hair, zipped back down for the next act, and then dashed up again to add blue eye shadow and don some over-the-top sequined dress.

When the prince rang the doorbell, my girlfriend took out a bunch of flashlights. She turned down the lights really low and asked Ali and Rita to pose together in front of the big walnut doors. Then she placed all the flashlights on the floor on opposite sides of the room. My job was to flash the group on the left on and off while she flashed the group on the right.

The prince and Rita's shadows loomed large as our flickering lights made it seem that a bunch of paparazzi had flooded the room. I loved this light show and they didn't seem to mind. And then they kissed us good-bye as Rita swished out the door looking like, well, a real princess.

Remember child's play? That means you do a simple activity with no demands. You get lost in discovery. You just enjoy yourself. You forget what time it is.

If you don't quite know what play is, think of a puppy. You know the profile: Wagging tail. Ready to run, wiggle, leap, lick. Many people are so good to their pets. They end up giving them the couch. Give yourself the couch for a change.

85—Eye on the Ball

Toss a small ball up into the air. Catch it. Toss it again.

 **MORE...**

Play catch with yourself. It is so basic and so satisfying. It is just you, gravity, and a ball. Delight in your natural hand-eye coordination. Give yourself a chance to look up at the sky. It's an almost sure way of falling quickly into the kind of reverie you experienced in your childhood but haven't visited in a long time.

86—THINK SMALL

Hold an ordinary magnifying glass up to anything you can find. A leaf. Your silk shirt. An orange peel. A sowbug. Your finger. The blossom of a flower. What do you see?

 MORE...

Just like a magnifying glass can set a leaf aflame when tilted at just the right angle, observing something familiar, up close and personal, can set your brain ablaze with inquiry and information. Looking at something carefully and in detail stimulates your sense of vision and opens up your sense of time. Time stretches out as you fall into the rabbit hole of details—the nooks and crannies of an acorn, the fluff and brilliance of a feather.

A whole world of tiny plants and animals is never seen by most people simply because it never occurs to them to look for little things in unnoticed places. To show yourself the power in thinking small, lie on the grass, roll over on your stomach, and poke beneath the grass blades. Put your nose right up to the soil and look at the earthworm castings, the wandering ants, and ping-ponging springtails. Look at all the colors and designs of things the big world doesn't have. And use that magnifying glass to see those things even better!

87—Let There Be Light

Light a candle and put on some music. Observe how the flame seems to keep beat with the music. Open your eyes a bit wider and focus on the candle itself. Notice its height, width, and color. Now focus on the flame itself. What color is it? As you look, focus on the color of the flame inside the flame. Spend a few moments observing the bright glow and feeling the heat. Now, simply blow it out.

 **MORE...**

Candles used to be the main way people lit their homes and places of worship. With the introduction of the light bulb in 1879, candlemaking declined, until the turn of the century, when candles enjoyed a renewed popularity. No longer our major source of light, candles now mark romances, ceremonies, and celebrations. They accent our lives with a warm glow of beauty and magic.

88—Rock On

Hold a rock in your hand. Feel its weight and warmth. Close your eyes and feel its temperature, texture, and solid form.

Rock On

When my dad was in the hospital, he was hooked up to all kinds of wires and tubes and monitors. He was covered with some kind of shiny blanket and wore a rigid plastic bracelet on one wrist. Everything was synthetic except for a bouquet of roses across the room.

I brought my dad a rock from the Colorado River. I wanted to bring him something of comfort and deep, essential familiarity. While he was sleeping, I placed it in his left hand, wrapping his fingers around its warmth and soft-edged shape. When he woke up from one of his drugged sleeps, he held it up in the air and said, "There's truth etched in this rock." He rarely let go of it. It looked so powerful and real in the context of the cold machinery and hygienic surfaces—a piece of earth created long ago from the heat of fire and the power of water and wind.

 **MORE...**

If you look closely, you'll find truth etched in every living thing, from tree trunk to seashell, from shark's tooth to feather. Hold as many natural objects as you can find and let their ancient wisdom melt into you.

89—Ice Is Nice

Put an ice cube in your mouth and let it melt. Or put one in your hand and watch it turn to water ever so slowly.

MORE...

The vast oceans make up more than 70 percent of the planet. It is always a good idea to remind ourselves that we came from the sea and that our own bodies are over 60 percent water. Try your own ice-baptism.

90—I'm Looking Through You

Gaze at yourself in your bathroom mirror. Make soft eye-contact. Hang in there past the moments of judgment and discomfort. Wait at least two minutes and notice what happens. Your eyes will not only meet those in the mirror, but your reflection will look back at you. Do you wonder who is doing the looking? Say hello. Invite yourself in. Soak up the sensations of deep recognition and familiarity and the delight and relief in knowing you're home.

Eyepatch Surprise

I poked myself in the eye with a poisonous succulent. Although it had soft edges, it oozed a viscous white juice that could cause serious trouble. I ran to the bathroom mirror and took a quick look. I could see a small hole punctured in the cornea of my left eye. It didn't hurt, but I was scared. I called my dad, and we zipped off together to the ophthalmologist.

The doctor squeezed some weird green goop around the whole eyeball, numbed and patched it and said, "You're real lucky. You didn't damage anything and you'll be fine." He advised me to rest and to remove the pirate patch in a couple of days.

The whole get-up was annoying, and seeing with only one eye was quite odd. Two days later I went into the bathroom, turned on the bright light over the sink, and pulled off the patch. I was stunned. For one frozen moment, I locked eyes with myself. My eyes in front of the mirror caught my eyes in the reflection. Unguarded, for one remarkable split second I fell into me. I think the trauma and the delight at being whole again cut through my habitual vanity and harsh criticism of how I looked. My protective shield was down and I felt like I was with a wonderful friend.

 *MORE...*

A mirror is a surface capable of reflecting sufficient undiffused light to form an image of an object placed in front of it. The etymology of the word comes from the Latin, *mirari,* which means "to wonder at," and from the word *mirus* or "wonderful." Once it was a wonder to be able to look at ourselves. But with today's insistence that we don't ever look right enough, young enough, whatever enough, mirrors have become menacing. It's time to take a risk and drop the judgments. Use the looking glass as a tool or doorway to enter into your eyes, the gateways to the soul. Look long and hard. Who's really home?

CHAPTER 8

The Last Eleven—

Mix

and

Match

'Em

These last eleven suggestions are guaranteed to get you out of your rut so you can get into your groove. And they only take five minutes or less! These combinations, selected from chapters 1 through 7, are designed to address special situations you'll run into as you go through the day. Some promote oomph. Others help you cool out. Do them whenever you want to feel and function better. Try them when you are extra tired, spaced out, anxious, or overwhelmed.

Check out all of the combinations and track your personal success. Discover what eases, what soothes, and what stimulates. Find out what increases your productivity, feeds your creativity, and tickles your fancy. Mix 'em and match 'em on a regular basis to keep tuned up and turned on. Be intuitive. Pick a combo that speaks to you right now. And if in doubt, always go for the Belly Breather Stress Buster (#54, page 109). A simple series of conscious breaths will quickly snap you out of autopilot and right back into living.

Feel free to change the order to suit your style. Some of these activities can be done at the same time. For example: The Calm Down Combo is Quick Snap: Click Your Teeth (#30, page 66) + Hand Web (#81, page 156) + See No Evil (#49, page 97). You can click your teeth together while massaging the web of your hand and then palm your eyes to end the routine. Or you can click your teeth and palm your eyes and then finish up with the hand massage. Try a few versions to find out what you love.

91—Relaxing Combo

Yawn Big & Loud (#17, page 44) + Bumblebee Buzz (#27, page 59) + Forehead Stretch (#61, page 125) + Hand Web (#81, page 156)

92—Energizing Combo

Crosswalk (#6, page 28) + Kick It (#4, page 24) + Upside Down (#50, page 99) + Open Heart, Open Mind (#79, page 154) or... just Jump on Your Bed (#83, page 162)

93—Focus/Problem-Solving Combo

Vocalize the Vowels (#21, page 49) + Infinity Eyes (#38, page 76) + On the Right Foot (#15, page 40) + Two Thumbs Up (#78, page 153)

94—Creativity Combo

Eagle Eye (#41, page 82) + Draw God (#74, page 148) + Think Small (#86, page 167) +The Right Hand Knows What the Left Hand Is Doing (#77, page 152)

95—Calm Down Combo

Quick Snap: Click Your Teeth (#30, page 66) + Hand Web (#81, page 156) + See No Evil (#49, page 97)

96—Sacred Tune-Up Combo

Fingers on the Pulse (#52, page 105) + Inner Happy Face (#57, page 114) + Prayer Hands (#59, page 119) + Head to Earth (#56, page 112)

97—If You Are Scared Combo

Shake It Out (#2, page 23) + Belly Breather Stress Buster (#54, page 109)

98—If You Are Angry Combo

Kick It (#4, page 24) + Fight Club (#11, page 34) + Belly Breather Stress Buster (#54, page 109)

99—If You Are Sad Combo

Facedown Touchdown (#14, page 39) + Rockaby Baby (#8, page 30) + Belly Breather Stress Buster (#54, page 109)

100—If You Are at Your Wit's End Combo

Spinning Windmill (#7, page 29) + Wild Hoots (#22, page 52) + Full Applause (#73, page 146) + Quick Snap: March in Place. (#16, page 41)

101—Your Call!!!

Snap Activity Index

To Our Readers